Moo

Jan Brodie

Moon Magic

ISBN 1 898307 81 4

Cover design by Paul Mason
Cover illustration by Dark Moon Design

First published 1997
Reprinted 1998

Published by:

Capall Bann Publishing
Freshfields
Chieveley
Berks
RG20 8TF

c

Contents

Dedication

To June, Elvina, Robbie, Johanna, the enigmatic Raymond, Lynda, Sian and Jinny for keeping me (reasonably) sane and for keeping my feet firmly upon the ground.

To my dear friends, Lee, Andy, Colin, Lou, Lynne, Andy, Allison and Carl, who always tell me the truth and refuse to pander to my ego.

To my children, Anthony (the patron saint of hair), Andrew and Joel; and to Mandy, my surrogate daughter.

To Gary, who has opened the door...

And to all those who have danced, sung, worshipped, laughed and cried with me over the years. Thank you.

Jan Brodie

Foreword

When I first struck upon the idea of writing this book, I did so with a mixture of excitement and trepidation. Trepidation, because such a book has not been attempted before (at least not to my knowledge) and in that the subject matter is so vast and varied; and excitement in the forging of a different path which has turned out to be full of twists and turns and a sharp lesson in deeper understanding for myself as the Lunar Lady has removed the clouds from her face and revealed to me yet another aspect of her magnetism.

During the composition of this book my own life has been changed beyond recognition. One phase has ended in the total annihilation of the life I had lived for far too many years and another has begun - a new life filled with love, truth and bright hope for a happier and freer future. I communicated with the Goddess during the 'Burning Times' and She said 'Trust Me'. So I put my trust in Her and She has given me lessons of incalculable wisdom and worth. I have emerged a stronger, and I hope a better person, from within the heart of the fire.

I have truly enjoyed the composition of this book and I hope that you in reading it will be able to experience at least some of the delight I knew as I wrote it.

Blessed Be
Jan Brodie

The Moon - Bewitcher :

I stared up Howling
And wondered why
The Moon shone so bright.
Then padded wearily through the night.
Her silver fingers caressed my back.
A gentle stroke to keep me on track.
Then I whistled down the hollow
Where her glance could not reach
A lover's tears on an echoed beach
A spark of divine
As she warms the sky
She kisses a cloud as her shadows float by.
And as I crouched by the river side
I saw her in rushes trying to hide.
A rippled edge and a glinting light.
I'm in love with a Lady whose home is night.

(Thanks to Dave Dwyer for allowing me to use his poem)

The Moon rises full every 29 days, 12 hours, 44 minutes and 3 seconds, and with her rise the tides, passions, romance, madness, crimes, despair, lust, violence and the birth rate of mankind and animals.

The Full Moon helps our crops in the fields to grow tall and tells all living things, whether animal, insect or human that it is time to mate.

The Moon governs the sign of Cancer the Crab and the mouth, brain, belly, intestines, breasts, the organs of reproduction, the right eye and liver of the female and the right side of the body.

We, as human beings are ruled by the Moon. Our emotions are manipulated by her gentle light, and the tides in our watery bodies ebb and flow with her increasing and decreasing orb. We rely on the Sun to sustain our bodies but the Moon causes us to LIVE. Primal and raw our emotions may be but that is the wonderful and motivating difference that lies between true living and existence. A small child will reach up, trying to catch the Moon with grasping fingers. A child knows the mystery of the Moon by instinct and struggles to draw her close. No child reaches for the Sun - it blinds and burns. The Sun holds no secret, no mystery, no magic. But the Moon ... the Moon is total enchantment, dreams and illusion and she is the lifeblood flowing through us all.

The Moon in all Her Phases

In order to understand the magical significance of the Moon and her phases it is necessary for us to also understand the scientific nature of her phases and movements. To plan and create a rite or ritual of the Moon requires us to have some knowledge of astronomy. In order to know her face and body completely we must also recognise her skeleton.

The Moon is the only body in our solar system which revolves around the Earth. Each revolution takes 27 days, 7 hours and 43 minutes to complete. The Moon is the Earth's satellite and lies 238,857 miles away from us. The Moon is closer to the Earth than any other planet, therefore, her magnetic pull is greater, hence her effect on the tides.

The Moon shines by the reflected light of the Sun and because of this, her appearance is altered as the lunar month progresses and the earth casts an ever-changing cyclic shadow over her face.

The period from Full Moon to Full Moon lasts for approximately 29 days. At the Full Moon, sunset and Moonrise occur at the same time as the Moon is in direct opposition to the Sun.

During the two days that the Moon is in conjunction or partnership with the Sun, the Moon's lighted half faces away from the earth and is hidden from us or we see a New

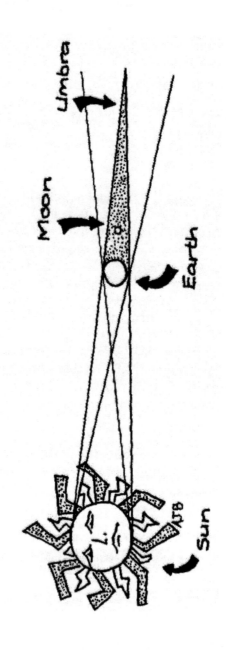

Moon which appears as a thin crescent. As the Moon waxes or grows she appears brighter and more complete with each passing night, beginning with a slender crescent seen in the early evening, which sets shortly after the Sun. About a quarter of the way through the lunar month the angle between the Sun and Moon is about 90 degrees, and we see a half Moon. This is known as the first quarter and she rises about six hours after sunset and sets about six hours after sunrise. As the Moon waxes or increases towards Full, both sides of her edge are seen to be convex in appearance. This humped aspect is known as a 'gibbous' Moon.

After the humped or 'gibbous' phase, just before full, the Full Moon rises as the Sun sets and moonset is at sunrise. During the second half of the lunar month the Moon diminishes through her waning phases, gibbous, half, crescent, dark and back again to New. During the Half Moon phase the other half of the Moon is illuminated and marks the last quarter. The last quarter Moon is also 90 degrees from the Sun but on the other side of the Moon's orbit from the first quarter. The last quarter Moon rises about six hours after sunset and sets about six hours after sunrise.

Each day the earth completes one complete revolution and the Moon is brought into view over the eastern horizon and is set below the western horizon. This pattern would be comparable to that of the Sun, if the Moon did not orbit the earth. From the earth the Moon seems to move eastward across the sky about 12 degrees every day. As the noticeable movement is eastward, the earth must rotate that same 12 degrees further to the east in order that the Moon can become visible to us. This takes about fifty minutes to complete and so moonrise is delayed by fifty minutes from one day to the next.

If the Moon, like the Sun, followed the path of the equator no change in the position of moonrise and moonset would be noticed. However the Moon follows the path, roughly, of the ecliptic and her risings and settings roughly follow the path of the Sun, but not in the same place at the same time. There will be several changes throughout the seasons. Because the Full Moon rises opposite the Sun, the Full Moon of the summer solstice (or nearest to it) will rise in the southeast opposite the northwest setting Sun. In the winter the Sun sets in the southwest and the Full Moon rises in the northeast, near the summer sunrise position.

Eclipses

A solar eclipse is caused when the Moon passes directly in front of the Sun and blocks out the Sun's light. The fact that the Sun is about four hundred times larger than the Moon makes no difference as the Sun is also about four hundred times further away. For this reason they appear to be the same size. A solar eclipse can only occur when the two planets are in conjunction with each other.

A lunar eclipse occurs when the Moon passes into the shadow of the Earth. This shadow is called the 'umbra' and extends into space by about 855,000 miles. The shadow is conical in shape and is always present. When the Moon passes through the umbra a shadow is cast upon her surface and a lunar eclipse happens. A lunar eclipse can only occur when the Sun and Moon are positioned in opposition to each other.

The Moon, Health and the Psyche

"An invalid, lacking in nerve health and vigour and a complement of vital force, should drink occasionally a tumblerful of pure water, which has been exposed to outdoor Sunlight on a bright morning or to brilliant Moonlight at night when the Moon is waxing towards its full; an exposure for 15 minutes will suffice. By this means the occult power of each luminary is conveyed through the water into the blood. The Sun is the father and is a great source of energy on the physical plane, whilst the Moon is the Mother, or restorer of nervous force, having a more intimate connection with magnetic attraction. To walk much in the Moonlight, especially during the second quarter, and at the full, in undeniably beneficial in some states of nervous atony (though it may be harmful at other times). The influence of the Moon on the earth is strikingly shown by the tides produced thereby, this luminary being magnetic, whilst the Sun is electric."
(*Meals Medicinal*,1905)

Science informs us that the influence of the Moon upon the human body and brain has a real and definite action and effect. We, as humans, are composed mainly of fluids. We function because of the passage of blood through our bodies. We can survive without food for quite a long time but without water we will die very quickly. Within our brains and bodies are minute tides which ebb and flow with the changing phases of the Moon; the tides being highest and strongest when the Moon is full. These minute tides affect all of us, although some people are affected much more than others.

I have a son, born under the sign of Cancer (ruled by the Moon) who is subject to greatly varied mood swings as the Moon passes through her phases. From babyhood he was restless and disturbed when the Moon was full and now as an adult he tends to become introspective, moody and withdrawn. Yet, over the years, he has learned to use the power of the Moon to his own advantage, and during his time of withdrawal he produces some of his best creative work, both written and through his art and photography.

In a few people the full Moon causes manic and irrational behaviour. From this phenomena we take the word 'lunatic', Oxford Dictionary definition 'Insane, outrageously foolish, esp. one confined as such (lunatic asylum, mad-house) of unsound mind; 'lunar' depending on or caused by the Moon'.

I know of one person who had to be confined to one room for the duration of the full Moon because he would set fire to his home and property if he was not watched carefully. It was impossible for him to exercise any kind of self-control against this compulsion. For the rest of the month he was a perfectly normal and well-adjusted person.

Crime, especially violent crime, is highest when the Moon is full. There are more murders, rapes and assaults than at any other time. There are also more hoax calls to the police and fire brigade. Crimes such as arson are more prominent too - in fact in parts of America, New York in particular, vulnerable properties and buildings are placed under special surveillance at the full Moon.

It is said that Jesus Christ was crucified under a full Moon and that Julius Caesar met his untimely and violent death during the same phase. The full Moon points towards a mass hysteria and violence that affects not only the individual but the group mind also.

For most of us the Moons phases will effect no more than what we understand as a normal monthly cycle of contentment, happiness and maybe a short time of depression or feeling 'low'. Many of us will not even consider that the lunar phases have anything to do with our moods and emotions. But the tides of the seas and the tides in man do continue to ebb and flow with unfailing regularity and we should be aware and conscious of their effects.

We need to attune ourselves with the Moon's cycles and by understanding them, we can begin to understand ourselves and what makes us function emotionally and physically.

Monthly Programme of Attunement

Firstly you will need to look up the dates of the Moon's phases in the tables given in Chapter 1. It is best to begin your attunement programme on a New Moon.

The New Moon

The phase of the new Moon is a time for fresh starts and new ventures. This phase is like a blank canvas or empty notebook waiting to be filled. Sit quietly outside, preferably after dark. It does not matter if the Moon is not visible. Clear your mind of everyday dross and allow the new Moon power to envelop you. Feel the stillness of the night and open yourself up to the lunar energies flowing around you. Sit for a while and enjoy the feeling of oneness you will experience. Think about the things you would like to achieve or abilities you would like to enhance or learn. You may also decide to cast away old and outworn habits and begin a new, more healthy lifestyle.

The new Moon helps to increase willpower. You may decide to give up smoking, become vegetarian, lose weight or just try harder generally. The new Moon opens up many possibilities for self-change and betterment. Have you ever wanted to write, draw, paint, create a garden or learn origami? Do you want to begin a new life altogether? The new Moon gives the impetus to make a start.

Make a commitment to yourself and the Moon power will fix it. Continue your quiet meditation each evening until the Moon changes to her First Quarter phase. Allow each passing night to increase your self-confidence and will.

The First Quarter

The Moon is waxing and growing larger in the sky each night. As you begin your meditation, she greets you as an old friend. By now you are feeling more comfortable and relaxed in her company. Meditate on how much you have achieved over the last week and thank the Moon for her assistance.

The phase of the First Quarter is a time for cementing your willpower. For many of you this week will be easier to cope with than last, especially in matters of diet and smoking. Reflect on your increasing abilities and be determined to continue to even greater things.

Be aware of your body - every bone, hair, nerve and inch of skin. Feel in your psyche the flowing of blood through your veins and an energising vitality coursing through your body. Feel your powers of achievement growing and strengthening as the Moon grows.

The Full Moon

You may feel a little edgy, emotional, excitable or uncomfortable during the time of the full Moon, especially if you are female. Accept these feelings as a natural part of your psychological makeup. Go outside as usual and attune yourself with the Moon's fullness. This phase marks the time when your previous two weeks work reach fulfilment. You begin to feel balanced and complete. Your self-confidence will have increased as have your creative abilities. You are in control of your body in that it serves you rather than you being a slave to it.

Emotionally, you will be 'on a high' and brimming with vitality. Set yourself a goal to achieve over the next three days. Other than this you do not have to do anything but sit quietly, allowing the pale Moon-rays to bathe you gently. However, in writing this, I should remind you that the Moon does have a strange and compelling effect on the psyche.

You may be drawn to dance in the moonlight, either alone or with others or you may find yourself chanting quietly. You may have an irresistible urge to take your clothes off and dance naked or just feel the moonpower through your skin. Do what you are drawn to do, and as long as nobody is offended, it can only empower you.

The Last Quarter

As the Moon wanes your time of communication with her will be reflective. Allow yourself, as usual, to attune with her diminishing orb. Spend this time of contemplation in considering your achievements over the whole lunation. You will feel physically renewed and revitalised and mentally more alert and capable. Your creative abilities will have improved greatly because you are no longer afraid of failure. You create purely for the pleasure of creation and are content in pleasing yourself. During this month of quietness you will have become, emotionally and physically a much better, more complete and happier person.

The Dark Moon

During the period of the Moon's dark (when she is not visible at all from the earth, just before the new Moon) you should continue your nightly meditation but direct your attunement to the night, its darkness and the Moon that is there, but not there. Enjoy the feeling of 'being' and communication with the universe. Watch the stars and attune with the vastness of space.

If it is difficult for you to go outside for your Moon attunements, or the weather is unsuitable, you may stand or sit at an open window (with the room darkened) instead. A period of ten or fifteen minutes a day is enough for enormous benefits to be felt or you may decide to spend longer on your attunement. Time is immaterial - your own psyche will set your own personal limits.

Lunar Waters

Lunarised water is water which has been exposed to the light of the Moon. This is most easily done when the Moon is full as the Moonlight is pure and uncontaminated by sunlight. It is almost impossible to prepare a lunarised water at the new Moon, for instance, because the Sun and Moon are in conjunction at this time, so your water would be equally solarised and lunarised.

Lunar water can be prepared by exposing a bottle of spring or mineral water (not carbonated) under the light of the full Moon and leaving it there during the hours of darkness. It is important that the bottle is brought back indoors before dawn to prevent contamination from sunlight. The bottle should be kept in a cool, dark place and a glassful of the water drunk before each lunar attunement. In this way the power and essence of the Moon is taken in externally and internally.

Superstitions, Charms and Spells of the Moon

There are many hundreds of superstitions, charms and spells which have their roots in ancient Moon lore. A selection of these follows:

The Moon and Children

> *I SEE THE MOON*
> *THE MOON SEES ME*
> *GOD BLESS THE MOON*
> *AND GOD BLESS ME.*

> *MOON PENNY BRIGHT AS SILVER*
> *COME AND PLAY WITH LITTLE CHILDER.*

A child born on the Full Moon will be wild, wilful and naughty and will be afflicted by many varied mood swings and changeable behaviour for all of his life.

If a baby cuts his first tooth on a Full Moon that child will be lucky in life and love and will always have money in his pocket.

A child born on the Full Moon will be strong.

If a baby wears a necklace fashioned from peony wood (a lunar plant) it will not suffer from teething problems.

The Moon and Weather

When the New Moon is seen to hold the Old Moon within her arms (when a faint shadow of the Full Moon is seen together with the New Moon) it is a sure sign that plentiful rain will soon follow. Likewise a halo around the Moon bodes wet weather to come.

The expression 'Once in a Blue Moon' is based on fact. A Blue Moon occurs very rarely but is a real phenomena caused by atmospheric conditions which cause the, usually, Full Moon to appear blueish in colour. Such a Full Moon was visible over Cheshire and Shropshire on October 9th, 1995. Because a Blue Moon is so rare it holds great power where wishes and wishing are concerned.

A corona or halo seen around the Moon is a portent of severe weather to come, usually rain or snow.

If the Moon lies on her back during her first quarter, she is said to be holding a great deal of rain in her curve. She will eventually tip the lot on the earth when she eventually straightens herself up (the Half Moon).

If the Moon wears a leaden corona it will rain. If the corona is red it will be wet and windy. If the halo is small it will rain. If the halo is large it will still rain. If there is no halo at all we can hope for good weather.

If you should point at the Moon it will rain.

'A Saturday's Moon
Comes it once in seven years-
Comes too soon'.

A New Moon on a Sunday is even more unfortunate. We can expect a severe worsening in weather conditions.

A ring around the Moon is a portend of rain or snow.

The Moon, Medicine, Health and Beauty

On the Waning Moon, boils may be remedied by staring at the Moon, spitting on the boil, rubbing the saliva well in and chanting 'What I see is waning, what I rub is waning', over and over again.

It is really quite obvious why this type of charm would be successful, and it does work. The rubbing of the boil will create heat through friction and the boil will then burst and the poison drain away. A fully developed boil bears an uncanny resemblance to the Full Moon. (Well it does if you use your imagination a little!)

Cut your hair on a Waxing Moon and it will grow quickly and become strong, healthy and luxuriant. If you want your nails to grow long and strong, cut or trim them also on a Waxing Moon. If you want them to stay short cut them on a Waning Moon.

An ancient cure for haemorrhoids tells how an afflicted sufferer should expose his naked buttocks to the Full Moon for nine minutes. This exercise should be repeated on the three consecutive nights of the Moon's fullness. It is said that as the Moon wanes then the problem likewise decreases.

If you can capture the Moon's reflection in a bowl or bucket of water, then that water will be charged with magical power which can be used to heal disfiguring afflictions of the skin.

Injuries contracted on a Full Moon will heal more slowly than at any other time.

If you should fall ill on the 8th day of the New Moon you will probably die. (so there you have it!)

The Moon and Luck

NEW MOON, TRUE MOON,
STAR IN THE STREAM,
PRAY TELL ME MY FORTUNE,
IN MY DREAM.

It is unlucky to see the New Moon for the first time through the branches of a tree.

It is unlucky to see the New Moon over your left shoulder, but lucky to see it over your right shoulder. It is luckiest if you see the New Moon straight ahead.

If the rays of the Full Moon fall upon your face whilst you are sleeping you will become mad, or at the very least, crazy.

A crime or robbery committed upon the night of the Full Moon is destined to failure.

It has long been reputed to be most unlucky to see the New Moon for the first time through glass (unfortunate if one wears spectacles) and the only way to prevent disaster, catastrophe and terrible bad luck from descending upon the ill-fated is to turn round three times clockwise and then bow to the Moon with great solemnity.

This superstition probably originates from aeons past when the new Moon would be greeted with celebration and ritual outside in the fields and woodlands. The people who stayed at home and did not travel out to welcome the Moon Goddess as she appeared in the heavens were thought to be most unlucky and were probably cursed by the insulted and indignant Lady. It is for this reason that we feel uneasy today about viewing the new Moon through a window or from inside a building. Racial memory is still a very powerful thing (and who wants to take chances anyway?)

It is considered lucky to bow nine times to the first New Moon of the year and then turn over all the money in your purse or pockets to ensure increases in wealth for the future. Money should be likewise turned over at each following New Moon throughout the year for continued financial success.

It is unlucky to argue or fight when the Moon is full or you will continue arguing and fighting constantly for the whole of the next month to come.

To see a coal-black stallion on the night of the Full Moon is augured to be extremely unlucky. Disaster can only be averted by meeting a fair or red-haired female by chance and bowing to her politely as you pass.

If you see a flock of birds passing over the face of the Full Moon you are destined to travel. This portend is most effective if it occurs on a Monday.

The Moon and the Household

It is lucky to turn a bed on a Monday (Moonday) and unlucky to turn it on a Friday or Sunday.

It is said that if you launder your brand-new clothes for the first time at the New Moon, they will soon begin to fray, wear away and then quickly start to disintegrate.

If you hang out your white bedlinen under the rays of the Full Moon it will be magically brightened.

Feather duvets, mattresses and pillows will lie more smoothly if they are turned and shaken when the Moon is waning and her magnetic powers are at their lowest ebb and therefore, weakest.

The Moon, Love and Marriage

Marriages have in the past been, and still are in Pagan circles, (excuse the pun) arranged to coincide with the Full or Waxing Moon, so that the couple's future life would increase in love, prosperity and happiness.

If a man or maiden was looking for a marriage partner, he or she would look at the New Moon and say aloud:

'Hail, Lady Moon, all hail to thee!
I pray you will reveal to me
Tonight, who my true love will be'

Then he or she would retire straight to bed and hopefully dream of his or her future partner.

If a girl wishes to know if she will marry, she should take seven holly leaves and prick into each with a needle the figures of seven years, i.e. 1996 in one, 1997 in the next, etc. She should next take a bowl of water which has stood out in the moonlight for the night. The holly leaves are then placed in the water. The leaf which sinks first determines her fate. If no leaves sink she will forever remain a spinster.

On the night of Midsummer (24th June) go outside in the moonlight and pick a red rose. Take it indoors where you have previously prepared a dish with charcoal and sulphur of brimstone in it. Set light to this and then hold the rose over it as it is burning for five minutes. At the end of five minutes take the rose and wrap it in a sheet of white paper on which has been written the name of the man or woman you love best. Fold up the paper and seal with three red seals. Keep in a safe place where it will remain undisturbed.

The most successful marriages begin on a Full Moon or a few days before.

The Moon and Travellers

It is considered to be very unlucky if a hare should cross your path when you are travelling out and about. The ancient Romans also considered hares to auger ill. Ramesey in his 'Elminothologia' of 1668 stated that 'If a hare cross a travellers path, he suspects he shall be robbed or come to some mischance'. Witches were believed to be able to transform themselves into hares so if one perchanced upon a hare upon the night of the full moon it could prove to be a very unlucky encounter as the witch would be going to or returning from an Esbat meeting.

To see a Crescent Moon which is waxing brings good luck for travellers (and lovers). A crescent shaped amulet should be carried by people who travel a lot to ensure luck and safety.

The Man in the Moon

Shakespeare in his 'Midsummer Nights Dream' called it 'This man with lantern, dog and bush of thorns, presenteth moonshine'.

Many people see the Moon's face as that of a peasant, often carrying a bundle of twigs on his back. He is sometimes accompanied by a dog.

Judas Iscariot is believed to have been sent to the Moon as a punishment for his betrayal of Christ.

In Panama, the man in the Moon was sent there as a punishment for incest!

If you look at the Full Moon carefully you will see the image of a witch riding on a broomstick.

A Full Moon Spell

You will need:

    1 wooden box, which must be new and unused.
    3 bayleaves
    3 scraps of paper
    1 pen (for writing therewith)
    1 white candle (lit)

Firstly, you should charge the wooden box under the Full Moon unto the art of magic by saying something like the following:

'Full Moon, Full Moon, I call to thee
Charge this magic box for me
Bathe it with thy rays of light
Lend power to my spell this night'.

Each of the three bayleaves represents a different wish (three wishes are traditional !)

Write your separate wishes on each of the three scraps of paper, one wish on each piece.

Take one bayleaf and wrap one piece of paper round it neatly. Mark the outside of the paper with a symbol that is meaningful to you, so you can recognise one from the others without unwrapping them and spoiling the spell. Chant each of your wishes three times and pass your wrapped bayleaves quickly through the candle flame as you do so. Place the wrapped bayleaves into the wooden box, shut the lid and secrete away somewhere safe where it will not be interfered with.

Now you must wait until the next Full Moon. If your wishes have come true remove the paper and bayleaf from the box, light your candle and burn both together in the flame, making your thanks as you do so. If one or more of your wishes have not been answered yet, return them to the box and leave for a further month. If you are still waiting at the following Full Moon, burn your bayleaves and start again.

Garden and Plant Lore

In both British and foreign folklore, the Moon is generally understood to influence the germination and growth of seeds and plants through her phases of birth, growth, dying and death. This influence is indeed based on some scientific fact, as the delicate and faint light of the Moon allows growth to continue through the hours of darkness, although obviously at a much slower rate than growth which occurs during the daylight hours.

Tradition has it that seeds sown at the new or waxing Moon will grow and thrive as she increases. Peas, beans and potatoes, however, are the exception to this rule and should be sown a couple of days after the full Moon. Many gardeners plant or sow seeds or seedlings on which the vegetables or fruits grow upwards; such as tomatoes, cabbages, lettuces and herbs, on the waxing Moon to encourage healthy leaf growth. Plants on which the edible parts grow downwards; such as carrots, parsnips, potatoes and radishes on the waning or dark of the Moon, to encourage healthy growth in the root and to maintain lesser growth in the mainly useless leaves and stalks. Farmers plant their crops at the waxing moon to encourage a fruitful harvest. Weeding and the destroying of insects and pests is best performed on a waning moon.

'Sow pease (good Trull),
The Moon past full,
Fine seeds then sow,
Whilst the Moon doth grow'.

Peas and beans are best sown just after the February full Moon if late in the month, or after the March full Moon if she is early.

Herbs, crops and trees should never be cut, harvested or pruned at the full Moon, but at the Moon's dark to prevent rotting and early decay. Apples and pears which are to be stored for Winter use should also be harvested at the dark of the Moon to increase their qualities of keeping. It is believed that if such fruits were to be harvested at the full Moon, they would continue to grow past their point of perfect ripeness and then soon begin to deteriorate and rot.

Cuttings, layers and grafts, because we wish them to grow and increase should be made on a waxing Moon, to enable them to gain in strength and vigour and to encourage them to develop quickly into sturdy plants. The waxing Moon energises them and protects them against excess wilting and stress.

Mushrooms should, if possible, be picked at a full Moon to ensure their best flavour. Mushrooms cannot be stored for future use, unless they are dried or frozen, and are at their most wonderful when eaten fresh from the field on a crisp Autumn morning. This superstition probably stems from the appearance of large, white mushrooms being visually similar to the appearance of the full Moon. On a Moonlit night, a field full of mushrooms appears like a starry map of the heavens drawn upon the earth.

Cabbages and brassicas should be planted at the new Moon on a Friday to keep them safe from frost damage.

Parsley seeds should be set at the new Moon and planted at night (preferably aligned in a North-South direction) or should be planted on Good Friday (or the first Friday after the Full Moon following the Spring Equinox) to ensure germination of its notoriously difficult seeds. It is said that parsley seeds should always be sown by 'the one who wears the trousers' in the household or the plants will not flourish. It has been known for men to destroy rows of parsley seedlings in the early hours of the morning so their neighbours will think the 'trousers' are worn by them and not by their spouses!

Folklore of Moon Plants

Moonwort, a fern-like plant with half-moon shaped leaflets on its fronds, is found on moorland and commons all over Britain. Moonwort is believed to have the power to open locked doors when it is pushed into the keyhole. It is also believed to have a powerful magnetism which will unshoe a horse if the plant is trodden on.

White flowers, which fall under the influence of the Moon, should be planted in the garden so that there are 'Moon' flowers blooming in each of the four seasons. The 'Moon Spirit' resides in these flowers and is most powerful at the time of the Full Moon. July, August and September are the most favourable months for contacting these spirits or elementals. These 'flower fairies' bring luck when they are glimpsed or contacted.

If you wish to plant a Moon border in your garden, try planting some snowdrops and Christmas roses (Winter), white hyacinths, pansies and daffodils (Spring), white roses, white jasmine and moon daisies (Summer) and white chrysanthemums (Autumn). A white-flowered tree would also be effective, such as a fruiting cherry. The traditional shape for a Moon border is a crescent or a circular bed which should be cut into the centre of the garden if space permits.

Plants and Flowers of the Moon

Plants which fall under the rulership of the Moon are classified as being cool, temperate, dry or watery according to Culpepper. Many plants that have white or very pale yellow flowers or have round, white seedheads, such as Honesty (Lunaria) are also attributed to be of the Moon's dominion. Melons, gourds, cucumbers and grapes, being moist, rounded and fleshy are the fruits of the Moon as are Lemons. Many Moon plants grow in or around water, many also have fleshy or succulent leaves e.g. stonecrops.

List of Plants Attributed to the Influence of the Moon

Any of the following plants can be used in the making of incense, and some in the preparation of Moon food. A pleasant and unusual Moon garden could also be created by the careful selection of a variety of Moon plants.

Adders Tongue   Whole aerial plant
(Erythronium americanum)

Arrach   Whole aerial plant
(Chenopodium olidum / vulvaria)

Bladderwrack   Whole plant.
(Fucus visiculosus)

Cabbage   Leaves, root and seeds
(Brassica oleracea)

Calamus   Rhizome/root
Sweet Flag
(Acorus calamus)

Camellia *(Camellia japonica)*	Flowers
Camphor *(Cinnamomium camphora)*	Leaves, twigs or crystals.
Chickweed *(Stellaria media)*	Whole plant
Coconut *(Cocos nucifera)*	Shell, husk and fruit
Cotton *(Gossypium barbadense)*	Flowers
Cottongrass *(Eriphorum angustfolium)*	Flowers and leaves
Cucumber *(Cucumis sativa)*	Seeds or dried flesh/skin
Dog Rose *(Rosa canina)*	Flowers
Dulse a Seaweed *(Rhodymenia palmata)*	Whole plant
Eucalyptus *(Eucalyptus globulus spp.)*	Leaves
Gardenia *(Gardenia spp.)*	Flowers
Gourd *(Curcubita spp.)*	Seeds or dried rind/flesh
Grape *(Vitis vinifera)*	Fruit (dried as raisins) and leaves
Guaiacum *(Guaiacum officinale)*	Gum resin

Honesty *(Lunaria spp.)*	Whole herb and seed
Irish Moss *(Chrodus crispus)*	Whole herb
Jasmine *(Jasminium officinale /* *Jasminium odoratissmum)*	Flower
Lady Smock *(Cardamine pratensis)*	Whole herb
Lemon *(Citrus limon)*	Dried rind
Lemon Balm *(Melissa officinalis)*	Leaves and flowers
Lettuce *(Lactuca sativa)*	Leaves
Lily *(Lilium spp.)*	Flowers
Loosetrife *(Lysimachia vulgaris)*	Whole of aerial plant
Lotus *(Nympheae lotus)*	Flowers
Mallow *(Malva spp.)*	Whole aerial plant
Mandrake *(Atropa mandragora)*	Roots
Mesquite *(Prosopis juliflora)*	Whole plant
Moon Daisy Whole aerial *(Crysanthemum leucanthemum)*	Plant
Moonwort *(Botrychium spp.)*	Whole aerial plant

Mouse Ear Chickweed *(Cerastium arvense / fontanum)*	Whole herb
Myrrh (Commiphora myrrha)	Gum resin
Navelwort *(Umbilicus rupestris)*	Whole plant
Orpine *(Sedum telephium)*	Whole aerial plant
Papaya *(Carica papaya)*	Fruit
Pearl Trefoil has white spot on leaf *(Trifolium)*	Whole herb
Pearlwort *(Sagina procumbens)*	Whole herb
Poppy *(Papaver spp.)*	Flowers and seeds
Potatoes *(Solanum tuberosum)*	Tuber
Pumpkin	Fruit and Seeds
Purslane *(Portulaca sativa)*	Whole aerial plant
Yellow Rattle *(Rhinanthus minor)*	Whole aerial plant
Sandalwood, White *(Santalum album)*	Wood
Small Burnet Saxifrage *(Pimpinella saxifraga)*	Aerial plant
Stonecrop *(Sedum album)*	Whole aerial plant

Turnip *(Brassica rapa)*	Root
Vetch, common, *(Vicia sativa)*	Whole aerial plant
Wallflower *(Cheiranthus cheiri)*	Flowers and leaves
Water Lily *(Nymphaea alba)*	Flower
Water Plantain *(Alisma plantago / aquatica)*	Whole plant
Watercress *(Nasturtium officinale)*	Whole aerial plant
White Lilies *(Lilium alba)*	Flowers
White Rose *(Rosa alba)*	Flowers
White Saxifrage *(Saxifraga granulata / stellaris)*	Aerial plant
Wild Clary, Sage Vervain *(Salvia verbenaca)*	Aerial plant
Willow, White *(Salix Alba)*	Wood and bark
Witch Hazel *(Hamamelis virginiana)*	Wood, bark and leaves
Wintergreen *(Gaultheria procumbens / Pyrola minor)*	Leaves
Wormwood *(Artemisia Absinthum)*	Whole aerial plant
Yellow Water Flag *(Iris pseudacorus)*	Flower and root/rhizome

Incenses of the Moon

The previous list of herbs and plants can be utilised in the preparation of incenses which are suitable for Moon magic, charms and ritual. The greater part of these these are easily available either from supermarkets, hedgerows, common land, health food shops or from your own garden. Gums and resins may be purchased at a reasonable price from New Age suppliers, herbalists or by mail order (addresses listed at the end of the book)

Incense

Incense is made from a combination of herbs, roots, gums and resins which are blended together and then smouldered on a hot charcoal disc. The resulting perfumed smoke is a very important factor in the effectiveness of ritual, and the consecration of talismans, charms and amulets.

Incense should be blended with meticulous care and attention, using ingredients suitable for its intended purpose. It is important to keep a notebook handy for jotting down details of quantities used of each particular herb or resin. It can be most irritating when you wish to make another batch of a good incense, and find you have forgotten the recipe.

Effective incenses for the Moon can be formulated from the list of herbs in this chapter. The most successful method

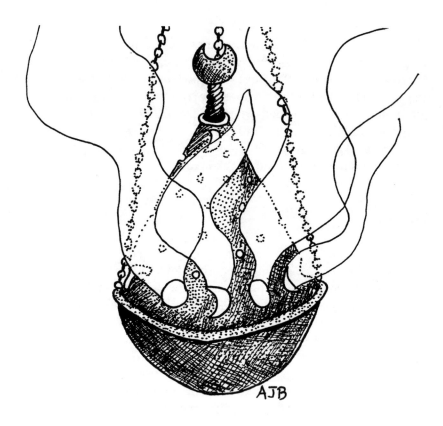

includes a balanced blend of herbs, flowers, roots, woods and resins. A purely herbal incense, though effective, tends to burn away very quickly. Roots and woods are slower burning and resins add perfume in addition to having purification properties.

Try to blend several incenses for different purposes, keeping them in small jars such as empty herb containers or even meat paste jars. Label them carefully. Keep your collection in a place where it is cool, dark and dry, such as a cupboard.

The measure used for incense should be kept for that purpose only; it may be a teaspoon or a tablespoon, depending on the quantity required. It is advisable, though, to experiment with very small quantities first. Multiply the quantities of successful ones later. I use a scoop from a tin of baby milk, being a strong advocate for recycling. Incenses can be blended in a special bowl kept for that purpose or in something as simple as a margarine or cottage cheese tub or a jam jar.

A pestle and mortar is a useful addition so you are able to grind ingredients down to a suitable size. Many beach pebbles are suitable for this purpose also, it is just a matter of taking the time to look carefully for a longish stone, which is rounded and fits the palm of the hand comfortably and then for a flat or rounded stone with a depression or concave face on it. For Moon incenses what could be better than stones washed by the sea and bathed in the light of the Moon.

Recipes

Experiment with different herbs from the list to formulate your own special blends. Trial and error is the only sure way to success. Moon incenses are traditionally white or very pale in colour. Ingredients should be ground to a reasonable size before mixing. A good incense should be carefully blended and not thrown together out of a handful of leaves and a lump of wood.

Much of the efficiency of an incense comes from the intent put into its preparation. The addition of essential oils in the following recipes is entirely optional, but oils do add that extra special something and serve to bind the mixture together.

Moon Incense No. 1:

1 measure	Gum Karaya
1 "	White Sandalwood
1 "	Wormwood
1 "	Mandrake Root (ground)
1 pinch	Camphor (a tiny pinch only)
1 measure	Ground Pumpkin Seeds
2 drops	Jasmine oil (optional)

Moon Incense No. 2:

1 measure	Myrrh
1 "	Eucalyptus leaves (ground)
1 "	Sandalwood chips
1 "	Jasmine flowers
1 "	Lemon rind (dried and ground)
2 drops	Lemon oil (optional)
2 drops	Sandalwood oil (optional)

Moon Incense No. 3:

1 measure   Guaiacum Resin
1 "   Calamus root (ground)
1 "   White rose petals
1 "   Coconut (dried)
1 "   Cucumber seeds (crushed)
1 "   Wormwood
2 drops   Rose oil (optional)

Moon of the Sea Incense

1 measure   Bladderwrack
1 "   White willow bark
1 "   Calamus root
1 "   Myrrh
1 "   Mandrake root
3 drops   Lotus oil
3 drops   Ambergris oil (synthetic)

Dark Moon Incense

Add a pinch of poppy seeds and/or black pepper to any mixture.

Censers and Thuribles

Incense is smouldered on a hot charcoal disc which should be contained within an incense burner (a censer or thurible). These can be obtained from new age suppliers/church furnishers or a brass or fireproof ceramic bowl could be utilised instead.

It is a good idea to fill the bowl with sand beforehand to dissipate the heat from the glowing charcoal.

Easy light charcoal discs are easily available. These should be held in a flame for a few moments until they begin to spark, then allowed to turn white (rather like barbecue charcoal) before sprinkling the blended incense on the top. Use incense very sparingly - a little goes a long way.

Moon Food

By long tradition, and evidenced in Dion Fortune's *'The Sea Priestess'* Moon food is generally very pale, anaemic and pallid in appearance. Ms. Fortune mentions clams, honey cakes and almond curd being served as a Moon ritual meal. Not a particularly interesting or tasty feast but having the otherworldly and unusual quality which is synonymous with lunar fare.

The Moon has a vast wealth of edible plants under her dominion and a varied and interesting meal can be made up from the simplest ingredients (See Moon Plants, Chapter 6). Most of the recipes in this chapter are vegetarian, but I have included an example which utilises white fish.

The food should indeed be as pale in colour as possible, but a Moon salad can be prepared from Moon plants such as Watercress, Cucumber, Grapes and Lettuce and served as a side dish. Simple dishes such as Baked Potatoes, served with cottage cheese or butter need no preparation instructions. White Marshmallows, although under the rulership of Venus, may be included in a Moon Feast because of their whiteness. Use your intuition and imagination to create interesting and unusual dishes, after all the Moon does rule psychism and creativity!

Papaya Salad

1 medium papaya (pawpaw)
1 bunch watercress
1/2 cucumber
1/2 crisp lettuce
lemon juice
salt and pepper to taste.

Dice papaya and cucumber. Shred lettuce and watercress. Combine in a large bowl with lemon juice and seasonings.

Potato and Poppy Seed Rolls

14oz. old potatoes, boiled and mashed.
1 sachet of dried yeast.
16 fl. oz warm water
2lb. strong white flour
2 tsp. sea salt.
1 egg white
1 tbsn. poppy seeds.

Dissolve the yeast in the warm water as instructed on the sachet. Cover and leave in a warm place until frothy. Place all the flour apart from a cupful, together with the salt in a large bowl. Add the mashed potatoes and mix together. Make a well in the centre and add the yeast mixture. Knead the dough thoroughly (a good way to rid yourself of frustrations!) until the dough is smooth and elastic.

Cover and leave in a warm place until well risen (at least 30 minutes). Knock down the dough, roll into a sausage shape with your hands and then divide into about thirty-five to forty portions. Roll these into balls and place on a greased baking tray or two. Cover again and allow to prove. When risen, brush the tops with beaten egg white and sprinkle with poppy seeds.

Bake in a preheated over at 200 C (400 F) Gas Mark 6 for about thirty minutes until pale golden. The rolls should sound hollow when tapped underneath. Cool on a rack and serve with pale Danish butter or margarine.

Honey Cakes

7oz. plain white flour
1oz. ground almonds
4oz. pale margarine, butter or vegetable fat
2 tbsns. clear honey
1/2 tsp. salt.

Rub dry ingredients together or process until crumbly. Add the honey and mix until bound together. Roll out on a floured board. Cut into crescent shapes.

Bake in a cool oven 150 C, 300 F, Gas Mark 2 for about twenty minutes. Cool on a wire rack.

Steamed Cod Served With Almond Sauce

1lb. Cod (or white fish) boned and skinned.

Steam the fish between two plates over a pan of boiling water until the flesh is firm to the touch.

Do not overcook.

Almond Sauce

2oz. ground almonds
1/2 pint vegetable stock
1 oz. butter
1 oz. plain white flour
salt.
A few slivered almonds for decoration (optional)

Mix the almonds and the vegetable stock together. Melt butter in a pan, add flour to make a roux. Cook gently for about a minute then add the stock. Stir continuously and bring to the boil. Add salt to taste. To serve pour over the drained fish, sprinkle with a few slivered almonds if desired.

Pasta With Mozzarella and Butter Sauce

Cook a packet of dried pasta shapes in boiling water for about twelve minutes until cooked but still firm. Drain and rinse with cold water. Drain well. Reserve the cooked pasta in a colander until required.

Pasta Sauce

1/2 pint milk
1oz. plain white flour
1oz. pale butter
salt to taste
1 tsp. mixed herbs.
6oz. mozzarella cheese (drained and diced)

Prepare the sauce as instructed in the almond sauce recipe. When cooked add the drained pasta, the mozzarella cheese and the herbs. Mix well together, reheat and transfer to a serving dish. Serve with Moon salad and poppyseed rolls.

The Crystal Ball

Crystal Balls are used for scrying or crystal gazing and are made from either natural quartz crystal or lead crystal. The natural crystal ball tends to be smaller in size, and expensive by comparison, but is much preferred by many people (myself included) because of its natural crystal energy. The choice of a crystal ball has to be a personal one, and the gazer should purchase the ball that he or she feels the most drawn to.

A crystal ball focuses the scryer's mind and aids concentration. The play of light upon the spherical surface of the ball fixes the attention, allowing the brain to produce images and patterns and often displays of colour. The scryer 'sees' with the inner eye as well as the physical one and the images seen are then interpreted through vision or clairvoyance.

How to Use Your Crystal Ball

Before any form of scrying is attempted, the crystal ball should be thoroughly cleansed. This is extremely important when the ball is first purchased or comes into your possession.

Firstly, wash your crystal in warm water with a little gentle detergent added to remove grease and soiling. Rinse carefully and then immerse your ball in a solution of spring water (bottled uncarbonated will do) with a teaspoonful of sea salt dissolved in it. Leave your crystal covered in this saline solution overnight. This process clears away any negative energies or vibrations that may have accumulated on or within your crystal and generally purifies it.

If you have a garden, place the bowl or container of salt water and your crystal outside and leave there overnight. If you do not have a garden a windowsill will suffice. This exercise is best accomplished when the moon is in her waxing to full phases.

In the morning, rinse the ball in clear springwater, dry carefully with a clean, lint-free cloth and polish with another cloth or a chamois leather. Wrap your crystal in a piece of black velvet or silk. A crystal ball should never be exposed to light (unless you are actually scrying) or to the vibrations of everyday living. NEVER display your crystal ball as an ornament or conversation piece, no matter how attractive it may be. The black velvet or silk should only be removed when the crystal ball is being used.

It is beneficial if the crystal can be exposed to the rays and light of the full or waxing moon each month. Place your ball in a spot in the garden where the light of the moon is reflected in it, and then leave overnight or for several hours. Try to retrieve your ball before daylight dawns. The moon-power is then absorbed into your crystal ball. It is also pleasant to find a secluded place in the countryside on the night of the full moon and charge your crystal with energy.

On arrival, unwrap your crystal from its cloth and cup it between the palms of your hands. Position the crystal so the face of the full moon is reflected in the centre. Hold your crystal up to the moon and feel the power flowing into it. You will also feel the power flowing through your hands, down your arms and through your body. If you wish you can ask the Moon Mother to charge your crystal and give it power, saying

LADY OF THE MOON
MISTRESS OF MAGIC
BATHE THIS CRYSTAL WITH YOUR LIGHT
AND YOUR ENDLESS FLOWING POWER
GIVE IT LIFE, THAT I MAY SEE
CHARGE IT WITH BLESSED ENERGY.

Feel the power once more pulsing and flowing through your crystal and your body and then make your thanks. Wrap your crystal once more in its cloth and carry it home.

NEVER allow other people to handle your crystal ball unless you are scrying or gazing for them, and then they should handle the ball for only a few moments before you commence.

Scrying is best done in natural daylight. I have found that dawn and dusk are the best times, when the light is there but is not too bright or intrusive. You should be able to see without straining your eyes, yet the light should be dull enough not to cast too many confusing reflections on the surface of your crystal. A crystal will reflect any points of light in its vicinity and this can sometimes prove to be rather a hindrance. Scrying in a darkened room, with just a candle lit for illumination can also be very effective and atmospheric.

How to Begin Scrying or Crystal Gazing

Sit before a table which is of a comfortable working height. The table should be covered by a black or very dark-coloured cloth, so it will not distract the scryer. The scryer should be conscious only of the crystal ball. Pass your right hand, palm downwards over the crystal for a few moments and then do the same with the left hand. This energises, magnetises and adds to its sensitivity. Relax, and allow your mind to attune with the crystal - to become one with it. Gaze over the surface gently, do not stare intently, this will only cause eyestrain and a headache. Gaze into and over the crystal as deeply as you are able, until you feel that it has become an extension of your psyche.

Clear your mind of all distractions, try to switch off your surroundings until only you and your crystal exist. A beginner will probably only be able to hold this level of concentration for a few minutes, but with perseverance the ability will increase. It can be helpful to play some quiet and relaxing music whilst scrying. This should be gentle and unobtrusive, but enough to take the edge off background noise and distractions. Noises can be very upsetting when the mind is in a relaxed, trance-like state, so it is a good idea to take the phone off the hook for the duration of the session. A sudden jolt back into reality can really unsettle a person.

I once had to have my nails extracted from the ceiling after the phone rang when I was in deep meditation!

When you have achieved the abstracted state that comes from concentration and relaxation combined, you will begin to experience dream-like images, feelings and thoughts. Pictures will appear, sometimes within the crystal, sometimes in your head. Do not be too disappointed or disheartened if these images do not manifest during your first session, or even the second or third. The process nearly always takes time, practice and willpower.

Perseverance is always rewarded eventually. I was teaching a class of psychic development students several years ago and we were working with the crystal ball. The students were progressing well until one lady complained that she was not seeing any clouding and colours in the crystal as she wanted to. She was hearing a man's voice and seeing images. The lady, unknowingly, was a natural clairvoyant /clairaudient with a rare and exceptional talent... and she was telling the poor 'spirit' to remove himself so she could see colours in the crystal like everyone else.

If you are a natural scryer, you will probably find that your crystal appears to cloud over inside after a few minutes scrying. This clouding appears mostly as a white or pearly-grey mist which curls like smoke through the inside of the crystal. Sometimes the clouding takes on shades of other colours which can be interpreted as per the list below:

WHITE	Good fortune lies ahead
SILVER	Very good fortune, relief from problems and difficulties.
GOLD	Prosperity, good fortune and happiness.
DARK GREY/	Bad luck and ill fortune. The
BLACK	darker the clouds, the worse the luck. Depression.

GREEN	Love, happiness and great joy.
BLUE	Good health, recovery from illness and healing.
YELLOW	Sickness. Problems ahead. Lies and deceit. Difficulties.
ORANGE	Quarrels, upsets, slander. A broken friendship.
RED	Danger. Trouble. Accidents. Take great personal care.
VIOLET	Joy and happiness to come very soon. Spiritual love and upliftment. Progress.

If the clouds appear to be ascending or rising to the top of the crystal the answer to a question asked is YES. If the clouds drop or descend the answer is NO. This applies to questions which are spoken or unspoken. If the clouds move towards your right hand or towards the right hand half of the crystal it can mean that spirits are close and help is going to be offered. If the clouds move to the left it shows that either the sitting is drawing to a close or that there is little more to be seen. The spirits are departing.

Symbols in the Crystal

Many scryers will never see actual scenarios happening within the crystal (like television pictures) but will see images or symbols which need to be interpreted. These symbols may be very simple ones and you must interpret these according to your intuition An eye could mean 'Open your eyes to what is happening around you' or 'Watch for a new opportunity'. A winking eye could mean 'Be reckless - enjoy yourself!' An Eye of Horus would represent a time ahead of spiritual growth and protection. A squinting eye could show the need for an eye test.

When symbols appear in the right hand side of the crystal they tend to be symbolic, i.e. a ring could foretell a coming wedding for instance. When the symbols appear in the left hand side of the crystal the images are more real and actual. These are things you will recognise (or your sitter will recognise). These symbols foretell things that are waiting to happen. The colours connected with these symbols should be carefully noted and interpreted. For example, a red ring could warn of a broken marriage or engagement. A yellow ring could warn of the coming sickness of a marriage partner. A gold ring would represent money, prosperity and happiness in a marriage.

In addition to crystal gazing for the shadows of future events, the crystal ball can be used as an aid to the vision of the spiritual. Meditation can be enhanced with the art of crystal gazing and the images seen therein used to further the development of the soul and psyche. This technique does take an enormous amount of effort to bring into being but is very worthwhile.

Crystals and Gemstones of the Moon

Clear crystals and white stones are under the rulership and influence of the moon. Sympathetic of her pale luminosity, white stones reflect the lunar virtues of motherhood, lactation, the sea, emotions, feelings, dreams, sleep, the psychic and clairvoyancy.

The moon shines at night, lighting the darkness and guiding our footsteps. Her stones are used for protection and instilling feelings of security after dusk and during the night-time hours, especially when one is walking alone in quiet and unfamiliar places.

Lunar Crystals, Gemstones and Metals

Aquamarine (Beryl)

Aquamarine is a form of beryl and is found most often as a light blue or sea green crystal. Precious aquamarine has the clarity of a diamond and is cut into many-faceted gems before being set into jewellery. Aquamarine of a less clear appearance is cut into cabochons for jewellery making, or is tumble polished or cut into beads for threading onto necklaces. Aquamarine is also available in crystal form or in largish pieces of rough rock. Any of these carries the same quality in magical or healing use. The magic is in the mineral not in the way it is presented or in the size, beauty or clarity of the stone.

Aquamarine is carried or worn as a protective charm when travelling on or over water. It has long been used as a amulet against drowning and seasickness. It is useful in the soothing of stomach aches and pains (the stomach being ruled by the moon). Aquamarine is calming and soothing and helps to heal emotional hurts and hardships. It brings joy and happiness, smoothing the pathways of turbulent relationships. For this reason Aquamarine is often chosen for an engagement ring. As a charm or amulet, Aquamarine is carried to instill bravery and courage and to keep the brain sharp and the mind honed to razor-sharp efficiency.

Beryl (Beryl)

Beryl is receptive and responsive. It is used most often to enhance psychic perceptions. Dr. John Dee's renowned crystal ball was fashioned from beryl and not from quartz crystal, as is often believed, and it can still be viewed today in the British Museum in London. Beryl is perhaps more sensitive for scrying purposes than Quartz Crystal but unfortunately, is not so readily available nowadays.

Because of its exceptional sensitivity, a beryl fashioned into a pendulum is a very useful magical tool. A pendulum can be made easily by fixing a bell cap to a stone or crystal or placing it inside a spiral finding and then attaching a cord or chain.

Beryl is a crystal of the sea and water and can be used in weather magic (especially of storms and rain) both to create and to protect against.

Calcite

Clear or white calcite is ruled by the Moon and the element of water. Calcite is used as a focus or centre during meditation and contemplation. It should be held in the hand or placed on a surface nearby so the full effects can be achieved. Calcite is useful for ridding the mind of 'spaced out' feelings. It soothes, calms and grounds. White calcite also attracts love.

Chalcedony (Fine grained quartz)

White chalcedony is ruled by the Moon and the element of water. It is helpful during pregnancy and stimulates the production of breast milk in lactating mothers. Chalcedony is a calming and soothing stone and brings restful and soothing feelings when worn or held in the hand.

Chrysoprase

This is an apple green coloured chalcedony and because of its colour is really considered to be under the rulership of Venus. However, it does have a strong lunar influence in that it brings into being that which is hidden deep in the unconscious or subconscious. It allows dreams to become realities and thoughts to become actions.

Marble

(Mainly calcite and/or dolomite, may contain serpentine, olivine, garnet. Marble is formed from sedimentary limestone which has crystallised into a soft, sugary rock.)

Marble is ruled by the moon and its element is water. It is used in protective charms and spells.

Moonstone (Orthoclase Feldspar)

Moonstones are opalescent and have a pearly sheen. They are known as 'chatoyant' (from the French 'chat' meaning cat and 'oeuil' an eye. Indeed, moonstones flash like the eyes of a cat when caught by a beam of light in the darkness. This play of light is caused by parallel veining or layering in the stone which causes a changing appearance when in different types of light and when the stone's position is altered by moving it about in the hand.

Moonstones are extremely receptive to magical charging and can be utilised in many charms and spells. They are 'feeling' stones and will absorb and reflect the influences of love, caring and emotional vibrations. Moonstones are believed to be more powerful during the waxing and full phases of the moon. Moonstones are often set in silver and used to make ritual jewellery and equipment such as wands. Moonstones can be 'charged' to heal menstrual problems and effect relief from excess bleeding or pain.

Moonstones have been used in the 'darker' aspects of magic, especially in committing and binding spells. They have the ability to hold a charge, whether this be of a good or evil intent.

Mother of Pearl and Pearls

These are truly gems of the sea and of the Moon and are extremely beautiful. However, they are not something that I would recommend for use in magic as they are organic in origin, having been extracted from the soft tissues or shells of oysters. This in itself is not a problem, the difficulty arises because the oyster has to die in order for the pearl or mother-of-pearl to be extracted from the shell.

If you happen to come across an oyster shell on the beach and it is well coated with mother-of-pearl, by all means take it and use it. The oyster has died a natural death so your conscience will be clear. It is actually rare to find a shell that has a good layer of mother-of-pearl inside it, so if you do find one take it as a gift from the sea.

For those of you who are not offended or squeamish about the use of pearls in magic, here goes: Pearls are protective and are used in love rites. Their reputation for being unlucky probably stems from the unpleasant manner in which they are gathered and from the many deaths that have occurred amongst pearl divers in the past. Pearls represent the Moon, water, the tides and the centre of the Universe. Freshwater pearls (from river mussels or oysters) have the same magical properties as pearls from the sea. Pearls are believed to contain the nurturing and protective essence of the Goddess and should only be worn by women. They are worn by women to ensure a happy and fulfilling emotional relationship and successful marriage. Black pearls are believed to bring luck and good fortune to the possessor of them.

Quartz Crystal

Quartz crystal is traditionally associated with magic, clairvoyance, scrying and healing. Ruled by the moon, quartz crystal is most often used in rituals and spells involving healing, love, spiritual growth, motherhood, scrying and clairvoyance.

Snow Quartz or Milky Quartz

White quartz is used in fertility charms and in all matters relating to motherhood and / or lactation. White quartz is also used to attain spiritual purity during meditation - it enables one to see and understand the truth. When carried as an amulet, white quartz serves to purify the aura, keeping it clean and healthy when a person is surrounded by negativity.

Sapphire

Sapphire, although generally a blue stone, is ruled by the Moon and is worn to enhance personal power and protection. They are also used to increase love. Sapphires are used in meditation and magic to both protect and to increase psychic ability. Sapphires work on the subconscious mind, opening it up and making reality out of thoughts and dreams. In magic, a sapphire can be used to create friendship out of animosity, it softens and smoothes difficult pathways and absorbs feelings of anger and resentment.

Selenite (colourless, transparent Gypsum)

Ruled by the moon and water. Selenite is a clear or clear greyish layered mineral which vaguely resembles calcite. It is used for creating reconciliation between couples and lovers. It takes its name from the Greek moon goddess Selene. Selenite is worn or carried to boost animation and vibrancy in the physical body.

Silver

Silver is the metal of the Moon, night and the moon goddess. It is the sacred metal of Isis, Diana, Luna and Selene to name but a few, and for this reason silver is traditionally worn by witches and those who worship the Goddess and honour the Moon Mother. Silver is also protective and is used to guard the body from harm or danger. Folklore has it that only a silver bullet or silver cross can defeat such creatures of the night as werewolves and vampires.

Stone Spells and Charms

Stones with a naturally occurring hole through them are made powerful in the light of the Full Moon for the three nights of her duration and are then worn on a cord by the sick to effect a cure. Holed stones (also known as Hag Stones) can be similarly charged and then placed in the bathwater or washing water of a sick person. The sickness then enters the stone through the hole. Such stones should be cleansed carefully by immersion in a solution of salt and water before re-using.

Hag Stones can be used as an aid to clairvoyance and scrying by holding the stone up towards the Moon so that she is visible through the hole. If you are fortunate, visions will be seen.

If you wish to see fairies, look through the hole in a hagstone on a Full Moon and wish hard.

Animals of the Moon

The influence of the Moon on wolves and dogs has long been recognised and documented. The Tarot Card of the Moon shows a wolf and a dog howling at the full Moon, showing that civilisation is but a thin veneer and the wild animal lies just under the skin in both human and domesticated creature. Anyone who has heard wolfsong will recognise the similarities in 'dog-song' too. This primal and eerie sound will cause the hair to rise on the back of the neck and a shiver run down the spine.

Many of the creatures of the sea are influenced by the phases of the Moon. Grunion fish instinctively know when the tide is highest and allow the waves to wash them high up on the beach to spawn. The female buries herself in the sand using her tail as a shovel while the males twine around her, and there she lays her eggs which are fertilised by the males. The males then shoot off back to the sea, and the females, after a long struggle to free themselves from the sand, wait for a wave to carry them back too. The next high tide takes the baby fry back to the sea. The incubation period of the eggs is exactly one lunar month.

In the 4th century it was observed by Aristotle (384-322 B.C.) in his book 'On the World', that the ovaries of sea urchins were biggest at the Full Moon. Shellfish such as oysters and mussels were noted to be plumper and tastier also. It was believed that the gonads of sea creatures grew and diminished with the the lunar phases. It was also believed that brains, as well as gonads and ovaries - both animal and human swelled and reduced in size in relation to the lunar phases. Modern science has established this to be true.

Many other sea creatures follow a lunar spawning pattern, including eels, herring, marine worms, crabs and scallops. Some spawning twice in a lunar month, once on a New Moon and once on a Full Moon.

Cats are lunar creatures, coming alive at night. Under the light of the Full Moon they cry their passion from the rooftops. The Full Moon signals that it is time to mate. Many kittens are born at the Full Moon also. Other animals which are under the rulership of the Moon are pigs, lizards, snakes and hares.

Insects swarm to mate at the Full Moon, especially mayflies and many emerge as adults from their pupae at this time.

The same mating pattern involves countless animals; bats, rats, monkeys, hamsters, worms, birds and people. Yes, humans feel much more amorous at the time of the Full Moon too. Everything that lives is in some way influenced by the magnetic pull of the Moon in her fullness. Sea creatures might know by feeling the changes in the tides, but land animals do not have that advantage - yet so many are affected.

Lycanthropy

Throughout the annals of time there have been countless instances and records kept of supposed 'werewolves'. These stories come from all over the world and especially Europe, where superstition is rife. Many innocent people have even been skinned to see if fur grows on the inside of their bodies. Others have been put to death, without trial, because another person has 'pointed the finger' at them. Such was and is in some places, the fear of the werewolf. Although all these cases and reports have been varied in content, one thing remains constant, the need for a Full Moon to enable the werewolf to transform into his lupine form or persona.

The Full Moon brings out the beast in many people causing increase in arguments, friction and cruelty. For some people the shining orb causes a shift in the brain which frees them from all inhibitions. I have heard of cases where an afflicted person will actually begin to behave like a wolf; howling, growling, rolling on the ground and developing an insatiable desire for rampant, continual and noisy sex. This behaviour continues for the Full three days that the Moon is fullest before slowly declining with her wane. Actual sight of the Moon in her fullness makes no discernable difference to behaviour at all. Even when confined to a windowless room the affected person will still act true to form. The magnetic and gravitational pull of the Moon causes the minute tides in the brain to rise at full flow and this effect creates a major cause of Moon madness.

As for the lycanthropy of folk tale and legend, there are indeed some poor souls who suffer from a very real medical condition which causes the growth of copious and excessive facial and bodily hair, including the hands, feet, chest and back; a thickening of the nails and a change in the shape of the skull which causes the teeth to become more prominent and the nose and jaw to take on a definite 'wolfish' appearance.

Popular newspapers have featured, only recently, the story of two young brothers who look like 'wolfmen'. Both having vastly hairy faces and bodies. These two boys now work as circus performers. How many innocent people have suffered or have been killed because of this sad condition and have subsequently died unnecessarily and violently? What I do know is that these poor creatures and others like them do not wait for the Full Moon to trigger the beast within them so they can tear the throats from their terrified victims.

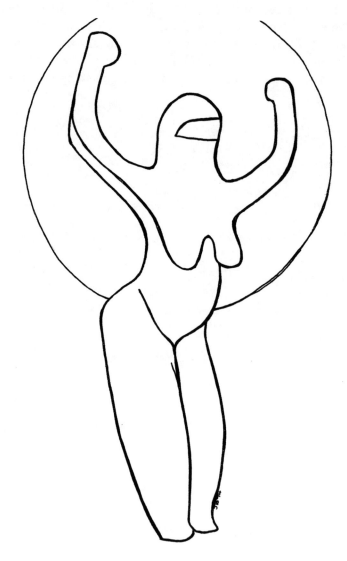

Neolithic Invoking Goddess

Moon Gods and Goddesses

Aah (Egyptian)
Aah was one of the names given to the God of the Moon (Thoth, Khons). He is represented as a man wearing the symbol of the Full and Crescent Moons combined. He is also a God of healing. Often represented as a falcon-headed youth wearing the Moon on his head.

Aine of Knockaine (Celtic/Irish)
Aine of Knockaine is a Moon Goddess who looks after cattle and crops. Her festival is held at Midsummer.

Al-lat (Persian) (Sometimes called Alilat, Ellat, Allaat, Manat).
A Moon Goddess who is considered to be the Mother Goddess, the female equivalent of Allah. Her rites are held at the New Moon. Her festivals are held on 21st November.

Anu (Celtic)
The Shining One aka Annis (the Moon) One of the Three Ladies of Britain.

Aradia (Tuscany)
Moon goddess and daughter of the Moon goddess Diana. She was sent to Earth by her Mother to teach the mysteries of witchcraft to the common people.

Arianrhod (Celtic/Welsh)
Arianrhod is a Goddess of rebirth and regeneration. Her name means 'Silver Wheel'. She resides at Caer Arianrhod, the Castle of the Silver Wheel, which is situated in the stars of the northern pole. Caer Arianrhod is the Celtic name for the Aurora Borealis. Her rites are performed at the Full Moon.

Artemis (Greek)
Moon and nature Goddess. It is said that when the Moon shines, Artemis is present, and all plants and animals dance for joy. She is associated with the Great Bear constellation (Ursa Major) and with wild animals being the Mistress of beasts and all wild things. She is a goddess of magic, enchantment and the psychic. Her rites are celebrated on the sixth day from the New Moon. Her festival is on February 12th. Artemis is sometimes a goddess of destruction, especially of humans. She is also a protective Goddess of childbirth. In appearance she is sometimes depicted as having the moon and stars around her head. In her rural aspect she is shown as a slim and supple young maiden, rather severe, wearing a short tunic. A hind or a dog is usually shown beside her.

Ashtaroth (see Ishtar)

Auchimalgen (Chile)
Moon goddess and protector against evil spirits and disasters. Auchimalgen cared deeply for mankind and was a great comforter to the people. She scared away evil spirits and protected her worshippers from disaster. If the Moon showed red in the sky it foretold of the death of an important person.

Baalith (Middle Eastern)
Goddess of the Moon, love and the underworld. Connected with willow trees, springs and wells. She is a predecessor of Ishtar.

Bast (Egyptian)
A cat-headed Goddess with a dual solar/lunar nature. Bast was connected with the Moon because cats can see clearly at night. She was held to be the seeing eye of the Sun God during the hours of darkness. Bast as the Cat-Moon carried the Sun in her eyes as she watched over the world using the reflected sunlight the God had given her.

Belili (Sumerian) (Also known as Belit-Illi)
Goddess of the the Moon, love, springs, wells and trees. She is also a protective goddess of childbirth.

Bendis (Thracian/Greek)
Mother and fertility goddess. Moon goddess identified with Hecate, Artemis and Persephone. Bendis had power over heaven and earth. She was once the centre of an orgiastic cult. Her festival is held on 31st March.

Brigantia (Celtic/British)
later Brighid (Irish). Brigantia is the Goddess of the New Moon and of Spring, she represents bright new beginnings. She is the Great Moon Mother and also has influence over the sea and rivers. Offerings of fire and water should be made to Brigantia. Her festival is Oimelc/ Imbolg/ Candlemas Eve (31st January).

Brigit (see Brigantia)

Ceridwen (Celtic/Welsh)
Ceridwen is also known as 'Hen Wen' - Old White One, and is the White Goddess of Graves's book of the same title.

Diana

Ceridwen is connected with Bala Lake in Wales (Llyn Tegid) and is wife to Tegid Voel, (Tegid the Bald) Lord of the Lake. She also resided at Caer Sidi, a place amongst the stars represented by a spiral. Ceridwen had a connection with wolves (a lunar animal) and it has been claimed that she is the Goddess of a cult dating from neolithic times.

Chandraprabha (Hindu)
The Lord of the Moon who is born after his mother swallowed the Moon. Depicted as a many-headed figure, seated in the lotus position of yoga.

Ch'ang-o (Chinese)
Ch'ang-o is the wife of I, the Excellent Archer. She went to live on the Moon to escape her husband's anger when she drank of the cup of immortality which is given to I by the Gods. The couple were reconciled, however, and I would visit her in her palace on the Moon. Ch'ang-o is always depicted as being a very beautiful young woman. She is sometimes known as Heng-o.

Circe (Greek)
A Moon Goddess who is skilled in the art of magic, witchcraft and sorcery. She is known for her evil enchantments, especially for casting a spell on anyone who landed on her island of Aeaea - turning men into swine or the animals which they most resembled, either by appearance or manner.

Diana (Roman)
The Temple of Diana is close by Lake Nemi, just north of Rome. She is a Goddess of fertility, childbirth and of wild places. She is a dual Goddess of the Moon and of living things. The festival of Diana is held on February 12th.

Djehuti (Egyptian)
Known as Thoth to the Greeks. Moon God represented as a black and white ibis with a crescent-shaped beak. (See also Thoth and Khons).

Ge (Gou)
Moon God of Dahomey (Africa) Son of the God Mawu, he is Lord of the sand and formed a triad with Lisa, who when feminine is regarded as his mother. The correct sacrifice to Ge is a white cock.

Gungu (Hindu) Goddess of the New Moon.

Hagar (Hebrew) Goddess linked to the Moon.

Hecate (Greek)
Goddess of the Moon, magic, riches, wisdom, victory, flocks and navigation. She is associated with Moon magic and enchantment. Like the Moon she is strongly connected with the powers of rebirth and regeneration. Hecate is a goddess of the darkness and of witchcraft. Hecate is Queen of the Dead, yet a strong defender of children. She would show herself to humans at night, accompanied by her pack of fiendish hounds; often at scenes of violence, tombs and at crossroads. Many statues of Hecate show her in triple aspect, as Maiden, Mother and Hag Woman. Hecate is powerful both as the Moon goddess and on earth.The last night of the month is sacred to Hecate and her festival is held on the 31st January, when offerings should be left at crossroads.

Hina (Oceanic) The Moon God of Hawaii.

Inanna (Sumerian)
Firstly an Earth and later a Moon Goddess. Queen of Heaven and Earth.Inanna is also called the First Daughter

of the Moon and the Morning and Evening Star. A strongly sensual aspect of the Goddess. She is known as Tamar by the Hebrews. Preceded by Belili. Inanna became the Horned Moon Goddess. The nativity of Inanna is the 2nd January.

Ishtar (Assyro/Babylonian)
Moon and Mother Goddess and held to be the daughter of the Moon God Sin. Ishtar is a goddess of fertility, love, marriage, divination and storms. Ishtar is honoured at the Full Moon. In addition to being the radiant Lady of the Moon she is an enchanting Goddess of sexual love and desire. She is the goddess who inspires adoration in young men, yet she is also cruel. In another aspect she is the goddess of war and battle. Her festival is held on 21st March.

Isis (Egyptian)
Also known as Aset/Wset. Wife and sister of Osiris. A goddess of fertility, marriage, childbirth, love, magic and healing. Isis is also a Moon goddess. She is also concerned with death and rebirth. Isis is the great, all-encompassing Mother Goddess - the All Mother.

Juno (Roman)
The sister/wife and consort of Jupiter. She is a Moon goddess and similar to Diana. A goddess of light and of childbirth - a new born child is born into the light after the darkness of the womb. In this aspect she is Juno Lucina. Geese and peacocks were her sacred creatures. Juno is a Mother Goddess.

Jupiter (Greek)
A God of light, sun and moon and natural phenomena such as rain, wind, lightning and storms. Known as 'The Thunderer.'

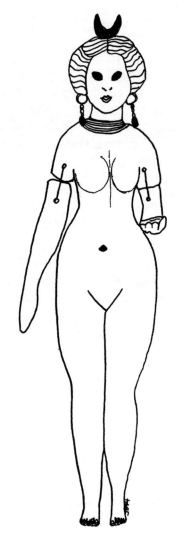

Ishtar

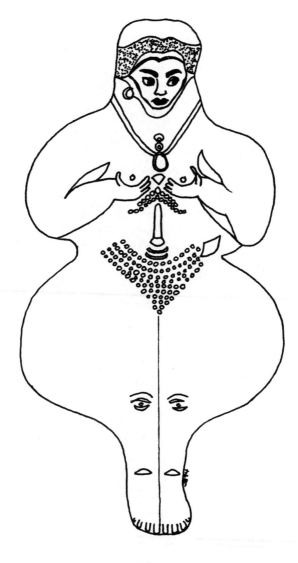

Ishtar

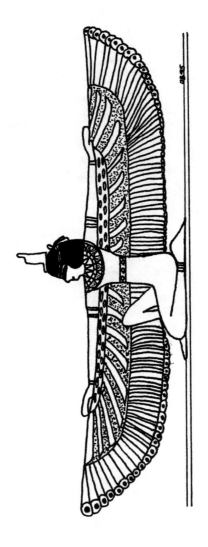

Isis

Khons (Egyptian) (Also Khonsu or Khensu)
God of the Moon whose name means 'The Navigator' or 'He who crosses the sky in a boat'. Originally worshipped at Thebes. He is represented as a young man wearing a skullcap from which flows a lock of hair at the right temple (the royal youth lock). He is crowned by a lunar disc and crescent and carries the crook and flail and a sceptre. Khons is also a god of healing and exorcism. As 'KHONS HOR' he is shown as a young, falcon-headed man wearing the disc and crescent moon.

Kuutar (Finnish)
'The Shining One' who is the daughter of the Moon God KUU.

Levanah (Hebrew)
Moon goddess. "Our Lady is also the Moon, called of some Selene, of others Luna, but by the wise, Levanah, for therein is contained the number of her name. She is the ruler of the tides of flux and reflux. The waters of the Great Sea answer unto her; likewise the waters of all earthly seas, and she ruleth the nature of women". (Aspects of Occultism - Dion Fortune)

Lilith (Sumerian/Hebrew)
Dark Moon aspect of the Goddess. Lilith is passion and sensuality - a succubus who fills men's dreams with eroticism. Whereas Eve is Adam's bright bride, subservient to him, who birthed children; Lilith is the Dark Temptress, ripe with sexuality, who menstruated and was dominant over him. Lilith is described as a 'maid' in *The Huluppu Tree* '...and the dark maid Lilith built her home in the trunk'. She could possibly have a connection with dryads. Lilith is depicted in the few steles representing her, as young, bat winged, with clawed birds feet and a conical 'witches' hat upon her head.

Khons (Khensu)

Losna (Etruscan)
Moon Goddess who is also known in Tuscany.

Luna (Roman)
Goddess of the Orb of the Night. Equivalent of the Greek
Moon Goddess, Selene. Her festivals are held on the 31st
March and at Beltaine.

Mama quilla (Inca)
Moon Goddess. Her likeness is a silver disc with a human
face. Mama Quilla is a protective goddess of married
women.

Mawu (Africa)
Is a goddess identified with the Moon. She is the creatress
of everything. She gave birth to a son, Lisa (Lissa) who is
identified with the Sun. Together they made a single God
referred to as the King of the Gods.

Myesyats (Slavonic)
Moon God. Sometimes appearing as an old man at other
times changing into a young maiden. The Moon is the God
Myesyats rather than Myesyats being the God of the Moon.
He is known as 'the Sun's bald uncle.'

Sefkhet-Seshat (Egyptian)
Moon goddess and principal wife to Thoth. Seshat is a
measurer of time (as the Moon). She is depicted as a
woman carrying a tally-stick or pen. On her head she
carried a crescent Moon and a star (sometimes a feather
also). She is the female equivalent of Thoth. Seshat is also
connected with writing.

Selene (Greek)
She is also called Mene. A sister of Helios (the Sun) and
Eos (the Dawn). With her crown of gold she illuminated the

Tanit

darkness of night. After her brother Helios went to rest in the evening, she rode across the skies in a chariot drawn by shining horses. Pan seduced Selene by assuming the form of a white ram and taking her into the Arcadian forest. Selene would come to the sleeping shepherd Endymion at night and allow her moon rays to caress him as he slept.

Sin (Babylonian/Hebrew)
Moon God who resided upon Mount Sinai. His appearance is that of an old man with a long beard which is the colour of lapis lazuli. His crown is the Full Moon and the crescent Moon is either his weapon or his boat. Moses is reputed to have been given the tablets inscribed with the ten commandments upon Mount Sinai. The tablets were said to have been carved on lapis lazuli. Is it coincidental that the god of the Old Testament should be described as being an old man with a long flowing beard who resided in the same place as Sin?

Sina (INA) (Polynesian)
Moon Goddess and sister of the Sun god Maui.

Sinvali (Hindu)
Goddess of the New Moon, pregnancy and easy childbirth. One of the wives of Vishnu.

Sirdu (SIRRIDA) (Chaldaean)
Moon goddess, sometimes called A, Aa or Ai. Wife of the Sun god Shamesh-Bubbar. She carries an eight-rayed orb which is her symbol.

Tanit (Carthage/Phoenician)
Moon and fertility goddess. The consort of Baal-Hammon and known as the 'face of Baal'. Her worship is known in Cornwall and the West Country as Tanat. The 1st of May is her festival.

Thoth

Telita (Babylonian)
Queen of the Moon.

Thoth (Egyptian)
Moon God and patron of literature, science, invention and wisdom. Keeper of the Divine Archives. Thoth invented arithmetic, medicine, astronomy, magic, writing and drawing as well as music made on wind instruments and strings. Also known as AAH-TE-HUTI. Thoth measured time into 'moonths', years and then divided the years into three seasons. He is shown as having the head of an ibis, crowned with a crescent Moon or as a dog-headed ape.

Tsuki-Yomi (Japanese)
God of the Moon. A measuring god who counts the months. A strong masculine character whose name is often followed by the word 'Otoko' meaning 'man'. He manifests in mirrors at his shrines at Ise and Kadono.

Virgin Mary, The (Palestinian)
Known in the Catholic Church as The Moon of the Church, The Perfect and Eternal Moon and Spiritual Moon. As with the Goddess Ishtar (there being fifteen steps of the Moon) there are fifteen steps to the Virgin Mary's temple at Jerusalem.

Xochiquetzal (Aztec)
Moon Goddess of flowers, love, marriage, art, singing, music, dance, spinning and weaving. Patroness of prostitutes. Her flower is the marigold. She is associated with the underworld and as a giver of children. Xochiquetzal is lovely, bright and joyful.

Interviews

Carl, Telford

'The New Moon - I am conscious of the Moon's phases without actually seeing the Moon, but when I do see the Moon, it lifts my spirits and I feel more fortunate when I actually see the Moon, that is, the sickle Moon. For me it is right, and I always start to formulate spells and workings then, and as the Moon comes up to the wax and Full, and I put them into motion just before the dark cycle. It seems to work for me one hundred percent.

The Dark Cycle... I am more in tune with the Moon when there is no Moon. I like the dark side of the Moon. Brick in the Wall and all. You are waiting for this aren't you. You are waiting for the one moment in my life when the only thing I can remember about that particular evening was the Moon. I can't say that it had such an influence on me that it caused me to strip myself naked and start running round a field, because I can't actually remember getting the kit off.

What I do remember is the Moon coming up over the hill, and the part when I said 'I'm being serious now' and I was being serious. If I hadn't been in a state of inebriation, I probably would have been able to remember the invocation. As the Full Moon rose over the hills and the mountains, she just popped up over the horizon, it was as if the Goddess was there and I was ready and waiting to accommodate her, shall we say. This was at the May Day festival at a place just over the Clwyd border. I have to say that I have never felt more in tune with the Goddess than I was at that time. That was amazing, because I was pissed as a fart at the time. Yet I can still remember it vividly. It was so good.

Sensuality, I have never really noticed. I suppose it has always been there on a Full Moon. Power seems to be more, for me personally, more enhanced when the Moon is on the wane, rather than when she is coming up to the wax and full. Mood swings, yes, on a New Moon I feel very lighthearted and creative and the Full Moon always makes me feel... I get feelings of ancient times, like I am born out of time and small snippets of memory come back. I get a longing feeling... a yearning not to be in this time, the twentieth century. I get a yearning to be in maybe the Middle Ages, maybe before that. I get a longing and that is where I want to be. The mood swing on the dark side is more positive, but by outward appearances to other people, I am obnoxious.

I am also more sensual and sexual on the Dark Moon than I am on the Full Moon As I believe it, the times past, the Middle Ages and prior to that, there would have been a village priest/ess or chieftain who would collect the menstrual blood, and as today we put the athame into the cup, the blood would have been used rather than the wine. It wouldn't have been drunk. I don't know. That is what I see, what I believe. I don't know if it works or not from that side of things. Because just prior to the actual bleeding of the woman, that is when she is most fertile. So I suppose it is the nature thing. I don't see the wine as blood.

It is like every other religion... it progresses and we need some kind of boundary and I think the wine was used in time instead of the blood. I haven't really researched or studied it but I believe the wine was introduced instead of the blood in Christian times, when Christianity first came to Britain. It would make an interesting study.

The effects of the Moon on personal psyche... it does affect me; I get more obnoxious on the dark side. I get very lively on the Full Moon.

Psychic powers, clairvoyance... yes, I have tried to shun it because I don't like to work like that. Precognition more so, I suppose that could be classed as clairvoyance but mainly from a personal point of view. For instance, if things are going badly and I am going through a bit of a sticky patch, then at certain times I get a feeling, a gut feeling, I will call it. I know that things are going to get better and that something good is just around the corner. I know it. I know what is going to happen.

The spiritual veil doesn't seem to be any different for me at any time of the Moon's phases or any of the seasons either. Even Samhain. I know that the veil is supposedly thin then, but it doesn't seem to be any different for me. It seems to be the same throughout the phases of the Moon and the turning of the seasons. Maybe that is just me and I haven't developed it as I should have done.

Mental powers seem to be more concentrated for me on the New Moon, for formulating spells, workings and such. I seem to be more lucid, shall we say, in respect of being able to put my brain into gear, think of things properly and analyse them properly without flying off at tangents, that is only the New Moon though. Maybe it works for me because I want it to work for me that way. It would be an interesting exercise to look into.

Louie Morningdew, Shropshire

I think the Moon affects me more when I am ready to bleed, especially during the build up to the Full Moon. When the Full Moon arrives, I become more alert, full of energy and I become quite aggressive as well. The build up feels like the build up before a period when I am ready to bleed. I also get that same feeling when the Moon is ready for her fullness. When it wanes it is like an easing, a relaxing, a calming thing. It is pretty powerful.

Even when I can't see it (the Moon) I know it is there and I know what phase it is at, especially towards the build up. It is so... it fills me full of energy. I get aggressive with it as well, but afterwards it just calms down again. Obviously towards the third quarter it starts to build up again until the Moon actually becomes Full and I go through the cycle of just being aggressive. I don't feel any calmness at all. It is quite an aggressive time for me. I think it always has been really. I feel more sexually inclined when the Moon is full and I find that when I do have sex around that time it is not a very laid back, relaxed type of thing. That also is quite aggressive.

I find that after the Full Moon, when it is going towards its First Quarter, I enter a resting period and I don't have a desire for sex for at least a couple of weeks and then it all builds up again. It is quite powerful actually. My husband finds it quite amazing really because I am more sexually alert around that time than I am at any other time.

I really didn't notice this pattern until I looked back over a couple of months and I saw how things changed. I realised that with the Full Moon I was more aggressive sexually and physically I was more... even with the housework... I would just dart about, get it all done and feel really, really good. Yet I still felt really uptight and obviously it is the same with sex as well. I am not there to please him at that time. I want pleasing. It is more for me, not him. It is a release in a way. More like a period would be. He is not the same, it does not affect him, I don't think in any way. He is more unemotional. My emotions are more on the surface, you look at me and you see an emotion. It is all on the surface, whatever is buried deep stays there for a long while and then eventually comes back out.

My PMT is stronger and more profound when it happens on a Full Moon then when it does not, there is more tension. I feel the Full Moon even when I don't see it. I don't need to look at the sky to know it is there. I know my own cycle and the Moon cycle as well. It all comes into one. I can't explain why, it is just there. There is no real reason why; it is there and there is a build up of everything and then a sudden release after.

Allison, Shropshire

My cycle ... when I put the studded collar on and turn into a rottweiler. Just before I have my period I get really nasty and I also become very selfish. I start referring to things as being 'mine' not 'ours'. I feel stronger at the Full Moon, more confident. I like to bask in the rays of the Full Moon as it comes through the bedroom window, to absorb the power. When I am basking in the Moonlight it gives me a sensual glow, I become one with the light and feel very energised and empowered.

When there is a Full Moon I sleep better, I am generally more relaxed as well. I charge my crystals under the Full Moon, leaving them outside in the garden to soak up the energy. When the Moon is dark I tend to dwell or reflect on people who have hurt me or done me harm and I feel then that I want to extract revenge more than I would usually, at say, a Full Moon. I am not really conscious of the Moon's phases when I can't see them, unless there is a New Moon and in the time coming up to a Full Moon, then I notice it, well, I look for it then. I love to see the Moon just when she is coming up and she is really big and has an orangey glow. I feel I could reach out and touch her then.

I like to lie on the bed with no clothes on and bask in the Moonlight. I suppose that goes right back to childhood when I used to lie in the Moonlight with the curtains drawn back. I never found it frightening even then. I like it when it does look eerie and the Moon lies low behind the trees. It is good. I feel much more sensual and sexual during the Full Moon phase. I like to twirl myself lustfully on the bed in the Moonlight (laughter) and thrash about in the silvery glow. I keep seeing the tarot card of the Moon flashing through my mind, with the dog howling at the Moon, that is it really, what the Moon feels like, the essence.

Gwydion, Shropshire
When the Moon is waxing and getting bigger, I have noticed that I am more susceptible to illness or feeling unwell. But as I approach the Full Moon the energies start to build and I become more emotional and I become stronger within myself. I tend to be more perceptive on the waxing Moon. I don't really know why that is. Probably something to do with balances, changes and the power growing from within, getting bigger. I notice things more, become more alert.

When there is a Full Moon I get very emotional, not always for the better, you could say I am a classic werewolf. I get angry and irritated very easily. I also get, how can I put this politely, very randy. My eating habits change as well. I tend to eat more red meat around the Full Moon and I eat less vegetables. This could be purely a taste thing, but I believe that it is the power of the hunting side coming through. When the Moon wanes, I calm down in a lot of ways, I get tired easily. I get sleepy and drowsy, I don't get into arguments and I get very depressed especially at the far end of the waning Moon. Within a couple of days the Moon starts waxing again and the feeling returns full circle.

At the Dark Moon I become very Gothic, I tend to wear more dark clothing. I tend to become quiet and introspective, not talking to people much. I can also snap. I seem to be a more powerful person and dress in the way I am thinking... very dark, very Gothic. With the Full Moon I become physically strong, whereas with the Dark Moon it is more psychic and psychological.

I can feel the dark energies coming around me, gathering up. I especially like doing things like going out on the Full Moon or when the Moon is dark, and just sitting there watching the shadows dancing round me. It is a brilliant feeling, as I have always considered my guardians to come from the shadows. In the dark people can sneak up and harm you, so when your guardians are of the dark themselves, it makes you feel a bit stronger.

I am conscious of the phase of the Moon even when I can't see it. Even as a child, when there was a Full Moon, I wouldn't sleep. I would scream and get very angry, throw tantrums for no reason at all. As soon as I was put near a window so I could see the Moon I would calm down and sit there watching it. This carried on until I was fourteen or fifteen years of age. If I was upset and stressed I would sit at the window and look at the Moon. Even on car journeys I would know when the Full Moon was approaching, by the way I would feel travelling, talking to strangers.

I would say that I have always been able to know roughly the phase of the Moon within a day or so. I would say I am more psychic on the dark phase of the Moon. I tend to have more visions, converse with ancestors, if you like to call them that, and I have a lot more dreams around the Dark Moon. The Dark side of the Moon is undiscovered territory. It is new things arriving. The same with the Full Moon, at the Full Moon my psychic power increases but in a more physical way.

I find that with my teaching and training in martial arts, I tend to specialise in kobudo and weaponry. It depends, on certain phases of the Moon I use more bludgeoning weapons, staffs, tonfa, side handled baton, numchucka etc. They tend to be a more physical thing, there is not so much skill involved. If you hit somebody with one that is the end of the situation. But around the dark side of the Moon it becomes more elegant, there is more thought put into it, more ideas for techniques, kata form, kata meaning a set sequence of movements, like a dance. It is ritualistic in that it is always the same and doesn't change too much. It becomes cleaner, crisper, more effective.

The Full Moon tends to give me more physical energy. It makes me feel almost invincible... like no one could ever hurt me. When I am running in a wood at night (for some reason I have never been able to walk) it is the beast in me I should imagine. I can always imagine myself in the place of a wolf or a hound running at night and you can see the Full Moon through the trees. It is a very earthy energy, very dark, very powerful.

I have for some time now been involved in role playing games, *Dungeons and Dragons* and *Vampire* being classic examples. The times of the Moon tend to affect my characters, the people I pretend to be, tend to reflect myself in one way or another, they tend to be Samouri, Elven or Japanese - very honourable people. If it around a Full Moon and I am becoming aggressive that is how my character will act, I will play them how I am. There will be more brute strength, more battle tactics, rather than common sense.

On the Dark side of the Moon (the Full Moon and the Dark Moon affect me the most) I become very devious, very dark very foreboding, checking things, cunning becomes a major part of the game. Also I find around a Full Moon I have a lot of trouble sleeping, I am energised. I sleep for maybe two or three hours and I am not tired. I am alert in the morning. It is a physical revitalisation. However with the dark side of the Moon I have a lot of strange dreams and astral travel.

Countless times I have been dreaming and thinking of situations, maybe martial arts kata, techniques in my head, and suddenly everything will change around me and I will feel a shift, a pull in my body and I find myself on an astral plane of some description battling out my own thoughts, but from a spectators point of view. I find myself using techniques against a six foot black cat armed with a similar weapon to me, for instance. A lot of the time this shows me mistakes in my own techniques and thought patterns.

Shelley (Tree Spirit)

I am very lunar - my god, am I lunar? I only have to be out under the stars and the Moon for ten days or so. If I am sliding away or if she is waxing or waning I'll get closer. It will call me on closer. My PMT, before Full Moon is worse. It is really, really bad. I think it is my age. When you get over forty you are fairly much in tune with your body by that time, you understand a lot more but you still don't listen to the signals. It is still hard to chase away a lifetime of conditioning of ignoring it. Sometimes, I am still going, 'What is the matter with me?' And when it happens I think, 'Oh god, yes, that's what was up.'

If I spend time with a group of women, again, in a workplace, for instance I work in a girls' school. The teachers in my department, obviously they are all women, and more or less now, I have been there four years, and we are all together now - all the time. Noreen and Jan, my other two close friends, we spent a lot of time together when the children were small we were always together and that was the same, we were pulled together in that way.

As regards sexuality, I think it does affect your libido enormously. I find that just after bleeding, once my first day is over and maybe my second day my sexuality is roaring. It is, it really is, and then before the build up and the PMT I have got no interest really. I am not in the mood at all, but then again, you know, my libido is going up and up and up now.

I take part in a small circle and we do have our own little circles as close to Full Moon as we can get them and to fit in with everybody's hectic lifestyle. We do find that when we cast our runes (sometimes we do runes sometimes we do cards) before we go out to get in tune with the Moon or what is this Moon going to be about.

Often, particularly towards the major, festivals, like Beltaine, we are all raging, but there is always an element (of sexuality) there. Always, it comes into the circle at some point, whether it be problems that somebody is having with sexuality or whether it be sharing a beautiful moment that somebody has had. We don't go as far as having sexual activity, but we express it verbally - definitely. It is a mixed group and we discuss everything. It is much better for us if we can. We are so hung up aren't we (as a race) We are so hung up, the British...

Rites and Rituals of the Moon

When working rituals with and in sympathy with the Moon, the phase of the Moon at the time of working a ritual both enhances and creates effect. In general terms, invoking rites are worked at a Waxing to Full Moon and banishing rites at a waning to Dark Moon.

The lunar deity invoked in a Moon ritual should be one who is in sympathy with that particular lunar phase. For instance it would not be fitting to invoke Hecate on a New Moon. Her influence is with the Dark or Waning Moon in her capacity as Crone or Hag Mother.

When working lunar rites and rituals, do not underestimate the power of the Moon (and the Moon Goddess). I once charged a moonstone in circle on the night of the Full Moon and invoked the Goddess with the intention of gaining enough willpower to stick to a diet for long enough to lose a couple of stone (my previous halfhearted efforts had crumbled after a week of privation when confronted with the sight of chocolate cake and chilli on a Friday night). 'What a clever idea' I thought to myself, with the smug assurance of 'One Who Knows'.

All went well for another week and then I collapsed, literally, with a pain in my middle. Childbirth had been a doddle compared to that. Off I trotted to see the doctor who referred me to a specialist. 'Gallstones' said he, 'It's an operation or a change in diet. No fat and nothing with legs', he smirked with sadistic satisfaction. I chose the diet and haven't had an attack since. Since then I have developed a yeast allergy, so I can't eat bread either. I have also developed an aversion to doctors. Wonderful, isn't it? I have erotic dreams involving platefuls of steak, burgers and sesame seed buns. I battle with bacon butty monsters on the astral. I sometimes think I can hear the Goddess sniggering and saying 'You get what you ask for, dearie'. Well you do, so think carefully before asking or at the very least specify a little more carefully and concisely than I did. Incidentally I did lose several stone but I have paid the price in blood (and a reasonable amount of self pity!)

Rites and Rituals

Moon rites and rituals should take the format of either

> a) A ritual to celebrate and attune with the lunar phases

or

> b) A ritual which uses the lunar phases to bring about a specified conclusion or to bring an act of magic into being.

With either type a circle should be opened before commencement.

Moon magic differs in many ways from Earth Magic. You will be working with the lunar energies and magnetism and therefore, the accoutrements associated with Wicca or Ceremonial Magic are not so necessary. I have found that it is enough to draw a nine foot circle, empower it and work quietly within it.

The power of Moon Magic comes from the inner self and through attunement with the Moon's magnetism and does not need to be generated through highly energetic dance and chanting. However, gentle chanting does help with the attunement. The energy is cool and calm rather than heated and frenzied but is equally as powerful in its own way.

The Moon power is directed through the channels of the intuition and the psyche, ebbing and flowing like the tides of the sea. Moon power is a living, breathing thing which should not be used lightly or without careful consideration and contemplation upon the work in hand and the effect and conclusion which you are desirous to achieve.

The Altar

A small table should be set in the centre of the circle or possibly a box covered with a cloth. On this should be set a candlestick containing a candle in either white for the New Moon, silver for the Full Moon, dark blue for the waning Moon or black for the Dark Moon. The cloth covering your table could also reflect these colours if at all possible. An incense burner should be placed near the candlestick with a supply of appropriate incense handy. You should also have ready the constituents required for your particular needs on that occasion (for instance a crystal ball or water in a dark coloured bowl for scrying or the herbs you may need for a charm or spell).

Moon magic is very diverse and there can be no set pattern for its many facets. However, I have given lists of which Moon phases are most appropriate for the performance of different types of magic.

Opening the Circle

Draw the circle with either your athame or a forefinger, and say:

> *I conjure thee, O circle bright*
> *To draw the Moonpower close this night*
> *Gentle light within thy sphere*
> *Guard and protect our loved ones here.*
> *Let this circle come to birth*
> *Between the Moon and the blessed Earth.*
> *A joining twixt the realms of man*
> *And the Lady of Moonlight, ere time began.*
> *Let us hold the power that we*
> *Shall raise within it, Let it be*
> *Strong and powerful, sure and good,*
> *A place of worship, truth and love.*

At each of the four quarters; East, South, West and North, should be placed a white or silver candle. As each candle is lit the following should be spoken:

> *Guardians of the East (or South, etc.)*
> *Be welcome.*

The business of the circle should then be conducted. This may be a ritual, a spell, a healing, scrying or meditation etc. When all work is finished. The Lunar Goddess should be thanked in your own words, and then the quarters banished and the circle closed.

> *Guardians of the East (or South, etc.)*
> *We thank you. Go now in peace.*

New Moon / First Quarter

Money drawing
Creativity
Pregnancy
Learning
Infertility
Friendships
Love
Beginning relationships
Healing
Menarche

Full Moon

Childbirth and Fertility
Healing
Scrying
Psychic Ability and Clairvoyance
Magic
Wishes
Love
Pregnancy

Last Quarter

Removing negativity
Ending relationships
Cleansing
Removing unwanted pregnancy (caution!)
Healing
Menopause

Dark Moon

The Psyche
Womens Mysteries
The Underworld
Deep Meditation
Cursing (caution!)
Sterility

Invocation of the New Moon Goddess

Maiden of the Growing Moon, Child-woman,
Virgin. Eternal dancer. Persephone. Kore.
Power of the New Moon. Brighid.
Rosy harbinger of promise.
Maiden of Spring and first love. Daughter.
Sister. Friend. First desire.
Energiser. Bringer of laughter and joy.
Bright flower of optimism and hope.
Cosmic runner. Hare Child.
Come ...

Invocation to the Full Moon Goddess

Lady of the Full Moon, Bright Mother,
Light Mother, Shining Mother.
Bearer of children. Diana. Ceridwen.
Weeping Mother, Bleeding Mother,
Goddess of Love and Lovers, Aphrodite.
Caring Mother, Sharing Mother
Confidante.

Sister. Fruitfulness. Fecundity.
The Universe, Crowned with Stars
Lady of the Tides, the ebb and flow,
Passion, Heat, Inanna.
Come ...

Invocation of the Dark Moon Goddess

Old woman, blood mother
Life in death mother
Ancient breath mother
Bone mother, crone mother
Reaping mother. Hecate.
We call you, Goddess of the dying Moon,
Dark mother. Grandmother. Morrighan, Nemhain.
Weaver of the cosmic cloth. Tapestry.
The threads on the loom. Barren womb.
Ancient wisdom.
Within you lie buried the secrets of ages
and the knowing...and growing
Wise woman. She who sees. The oracle.
The spell. Enchantment.
Spider on the Web of Life.
Come...

Rituals to Celebrate the Female Rites of Passage

The following rituals are formulated for celebration by women only. Under no circumstances should any male be admitted to the circle.

The Menarche

The menarche, or first menstruation of a young girl, is a time to be celebrated rather than disregarded and hidden away. The issue of first blood initiates the girl into the mystic sisterhood of women. For a young girl the menarche can be a frightening, confusing and embarrassing time, a horror furtively discussed in school changing rooms. She may be as young as ten years or as old as fifteen or sixteen when the first bleeding occurs. Whatever her age, the bleeding marks the transition which changes her physically from a child to a woman capable of bearing children and this should be treated with the understanding reverence it deserves.

Preparation

This rite should be celebrated on a New to Waxing Moon. The circle and altar should be decorated with as much red as possible, such as red flowers, ribbons and candles. Red being the feminine colour of life and of blood. Food and wine should also be red and include apples and a pomegranate (if in season). Clothing should also be red. Each woman present should have prepared a gift for the girl to mark her transition from child to woman; these gifts should again be either red in colour or have lunar symbolism as she is now under the dominion of the Moon. Suitable gifts might include a piece of jewellery in silver and moonstone, a bouquet of red roses (either real or silk) or possibly an item of red clothing.

The girl should select for herself two items to represent her transition from child to woman; one to symbolise childhood (such as a toy) and one to symbolise womanhood.
These should be brought with her to the circle.

The Rite

A circle is drawn and empowered by the women present. The girl and an older woman remain outside it. A red cord is laid on the floor, just inside the circle, to represent the crossing over from girlhood to womanhood. The other women form a semi-circle around the edges of the circle with the Priestess or officiating woman standing in the centre of the circle.

Priestess:: *We are gathered here to bring a new member into the Sisterhood of Women. Outside this circle stands ....name.......... We welcome her with love. Come forward to join us now, leaving childhood behind.*

The girl enters the circle, led by the older woman. She places her symbol of childhood on the floor at the edge of the circle and then steps over the cord. Her symbol of womanhood is laid on the floor in front of the cord. The Priestess steps forward and embraces the girl, welcoming her. The other women then embrace the girl in turn. The whole group should then sit on the floor, forming a circle with hands joined (including the girl).

Priestess: *Thus we link with the spirit of womanhood. Childhood is left behind. ....name...... is now a woman, and as a woman, carries with her the potential of new life and the continuity of humankind upon the earth. She is indeed blessed. May the Goddess smile upon her and guide her future path.*

Women: *Welcome ....name.......... to the sisterhood of women.*

May the Goddess guide you and keep you.

Girl: *No curse this, for I am blessed with the promise of future life. I see myself strong and proud - a sister. If I choose, I shall be a mother in a future time. But until then, these, my sisters, shall teach me. In these women I put my trust.*

Women: *So it shall be. And rightly so.*

The women then offer the girl their gifts and the gathering becomes more informal. At this time any worries or questions that the girl may have are dealt with. She should be encouraged to share any apprehensions and to overcome any possible shyness. It is important that she feels relaxed and at ease.

Stories and anecdotes relating to menstruation could be told (but should not be alarming in any way). Food and wine are shared. If pomegranates are in season, one should be broken and the seeds shared as a representation of the many times that the girl will menstruate during her future fertile years. The circle should be closed when the Priestess feels ready.

The Menopause

For many women this phase of life is met with apprehension and a sense of loss. To some these feelings almost equal bereavement. Yes, childbearing days are over but this is something which should be met with joy not regret. This may be difficult for many women to accept, especially those who have never borne children, yet wanted them badly, and not through choice, for it must be every woman's right to choose whether or not she brings a child into the world or not.

Accept it she must - there is no other option. The biological clocks ticks inexorably onwards. The menopause brings many physical and psychological changes with it. A woman may feel less feminine when she ceases to ovulate or she may feel redundant and useless. The menopause must be looked at as a positive thing. Yes, it signifies the ending of a phase of life but it also marks the beginning of a new one.

The menopause can occur at any time between about thirty-five years and fifty (with variations either way) which by any standards does not signify old age. Women tend to live longer than men so the menopausal woman still has many years in which to fulfil her dreams and ambitions. She is freed from the worry of pregnancy, so can enjoy the pleasure of lovemaking for it's own sake.

She is likely to find also that her libido increases significantly. Her children (if she has children) will have flown the nest or be of an age to be reasonably independent. Her time is becoming much less structured towards other people and more towards her own needs and desires.

Preparation

The rite should be performed on a waning to dark Moon. The circle should be prepared and decorated with flowers and ribbons in white, red and black. There should be three candles upon the altar, unlit. These should also be white, red and black, to represent the three aspects of the Goddess and the three life-stages of women.

All the women present should have prepared gifts for the woman for whom the ritual is being enacted. These gifts should be carefully chosen to reflect her personality or future ambitions. There should also be three photographs of the woman at various stages of her life. One at around puberty, one when pregnant or at sexual maturity (as a bride, maybe) and one that is quite recent.

These photographs will be used for attunement purposes during the ritual.

A black cord is laid across the edge of the circle.

The RIte:

The circle is drawn and empowered by the women present. The woman for whom the ritual is being conducted remains outside the circle until she is called in by the Priestess or officiating woman. The women inside the circle form a horseshoe around the edges facing the woman.

Priestess: *This gathering of sisters comes together tonight to mark the passage of ....name........ through her menopause. Let her join with us now.*

Woman: Enters the circle and steps over the cord.

*I cross this bridge to join my sisters with joy
in my heart. This cord marks the passage
from one phase of life to the next.*

Priestess: *Welcome.*

Now light the candles which mark the passing of time. One
for the Maiden, one for the Mother and one for The Lady of
Wisdom.

The woman lights each candle in turn at the altar, then
returns to join the other women. They then sit down in a
circle on the floor.

The menopause brings many changes, some are difficult to
cope with, some are positive and bring bright blessings with
them. Look at these photographs now, and relive the past.
Feel in your heart and soul how you felt then, and let us
share in your life and experience.

The woman takes the first photograph and tells her story.
The other women then join in by telling their experiences of
that time in their lives. This continues with the second
photograph. The third photograph relates to the present
and future, and here the woman may express her apprehensions and doubts as well as her hopes and ambitions.
Older women present can relate their experiences.

When this part of the rite is concluded the women share
wine and food and their gifts are presented to the woman.

The circle is closed when the Priestess feels it is appropriate.

Similar rituals may be formulated for pregnancy, childbirth and even the loss of virginity. It is important for women to work together as a sisterhood. This strengthens bonds of friendship, mutual trust and enriches the lives of all the women involved.

Astrological Moon Signs

In a natal astrology chart (a map of the sky at the precise moment of birth) the position of the Moon is of great importance. The Moon sign signifies how we react and interrelate emotionally in all areas of our lives.

Our Sun sign and Ascendant show our personality and the persona we show to the world but our Moon sign is connected with our deep subconscious and the psyche. To find out what your Moon sign is check your date of birth in any astrological ephemeris.

Moon in Aries

Aries Moon people have a deep desire to lead and to be followed - in fact they expect no less from other people. Material power is very important to them as are the trappings and luxuries associated with such.

Aries Moons are snappy, short-tempered, irritable, argumentative, domineering and difficult at times. They can devastate other people with their vitriolic, sharp and tactless remarks. On the other hand they can be witty, charming and original in thought and action. Calmness is not an Aries Moon attribute; they can become excited and keyed-up without provocation. The occult holds much interest for them and they often have the gift of clairvoyance. In matters of love and romance, the Aries Moon is passionate and exciting as a lover. They are never afraid to try anything! However, much of the thrill for Aries Moons is in the chase, once the quarry has been captured the Aries Moon may lose interest quite rapidly. Aries Moons are natural hunters and adventurers so much of the fun is in the hunt itself rather than the capture.

Emotionally the Aries Moon tends to dominate others and can become quite huffy when crossed. These leaders expect everyone to follow them without question. On a positive note, the Aries Moon can have an iron willpower and will succeed when others fail miserably. Danger means nothing to them, in fact they thrive on it. They are brimming with ideas and initiative and are able to make their plans into reality. Their instincts can be relied on and they rarely take the advice of other people, much preferring to act on their own intuition which they rarely question.

Moon in Taurus

The Moon is exalted in Taurus and these people are usually well-blessed with life's material comforts. Material things are of importance to these people; they need to be comfortable. Taurus Moons are reliable, steady people who don't take chances on a whim. However, they can also be impressionable and strive for the possession of things which are beyond their means. They are generally careful with their money and have a tendency to save more than they spend. Material security is important to them.

Taurus Moons are good listeners and will draw troubled people to them when practical advice is necessary. They are naturally sympathetic and kind-hearted. They don't make snap decisions, preferring to think things over carefully before reaching a decision. As regards family, Taurus Moons can be over-protective and fussy. They expect their children to achieve.

Taurus Moons are very physical people who have a great love for comfort, food, drink and sex. Many over-indulge in everything, which can lead to health problems. The senses of touch and taste are very well developed. Some Taurus Moons can be boringly conservative and lazy or they may be emotionally clinging, which can cause relationship difficulties.

Moon in Gemini

Moon in Gemini people are free-spirited and refuse to be tied or pinned down. They are independent, witty, charming, lively and fun to be with. Gemini Moons are clever, knowing something about everything, although not always in great depth.

Gemini Moons are popular people as they have such verve for life and living. They are very active, both mentally and physically, enjoying a varied social life. They enjoy conversation and talking very much and are natural mimics. These people are able to store information in their computer-like memories and retrieve it on demand. Too much solitude can cause problems as they need the stimulation of other people and activity to keep them emotionally healthy. Gemini Moons enjoy teasing other people and 'stirring', just for the pleasure of it, although they are not deliberately malicious and nasty. In fact they will run away from emotional tangles and pain rather than face up to it.

In love, Gemini Moons require much more than a pretty face to keep their interest. Brains and intellectual stimulation are much more necessary to keep their interest - boredom sets in very quickly. Gemini Moons can lie both effectively and efficiently and they like to make up stories - sometimes reality and fantasy can become over-entwined.

Moon in Cancer

The Moon is at home in Cancer. Moon in Cancer people need harmony, peace and tenderness in order to be truly happy. These people see beauty in many things and are very much attuned to their surroundings. The Moon in Cancer bestows an extremely impressionable nature and a hypersensitivity to atmospheres, whether these be good or difficult. Conflict and uncertainty will cause great emotional pain and distress. The Cancerian habit of withdrawing when difficulties arise is strong here. Time is needed for thought and assimilation before decisions and conclusions are reached.

Cancerian Moons enjoy comfort, ease and thrive in the company of like-minded people. They enjoy good conversation and tend to keep their friends from childhood. Mood swings can cause problems as these people are much affected by the Moon herself, so they can be very 'up' and then very 'down' almost instantly.

Emotionally, they need to be loved and need constant reassurance from their loved ones that they are cared for. Cancerian Moons are naturally very psychic and 'pick up' vibrations from all around them. Their intuition can be relied upon as they are feeling rather than thinking people. Some Cancerian Moons can be lazy, mentally inert and over-impressionable. They can also lack in responsibility, both for themselves and for other people, drifting through life without any real plans or thought for the future.

Moon in Leo

The Moon in Leo brings a natural sense of drama and a certain flamboyance with it. Moon in Leo people need to be admired, adored even, by other people, especially loved ones. If this adoration is not forthcoming, they will withdraw to sulk and lick their (mainly imagined) wounds. They can be arrogant, conceited, theatrical, proud, pompous and overbearing yet they can also be self-sacrificing and uphold their obligations. Their word is their bond.

Leo Moons have warm and generous personalities and attract friends easily to themselves. Deep inside the Leo Moon suffers from hidden insecurities which are covered up by their outward personality-and-a-half. Leo Moons are generally positive and can make decisions. They look forward with hope and optimism, never being kept down for very long.

In love Leo Moons are passionate and can be smothering after a time, being easily roused to jealousy and possessiveness. Leo Moons have expensive tastes, preferring the best that money can buy, and they care about their appearance.

Moon in Virgo

The Moon in Virgo bestows sense, practicality, efficiency and intelligence. These people work hard to achieve success and are trustworthy. Moon in Virgos are naturally quite reserved and some can lack in confidence.

Health matters are generally of great importance and Virgo Moons can be very fussy eaters. Some can be health conscious to the point of hypochondria. They are also fastidious about hygiene and cleanliness both personally and about the home, which is usually neat and spotless. This is achieved seemingly without a great deal of effort, it is a natural ability which combines well with the inherent efficiency of this sign.

In love Virgo Moons are mental rather than physical people and tend to analyse relationships rather too deeply. Attraction comes through the intellect rather than just the body. Passions become a mental thing connected with thought.

Many are attracted by erotica in the written word. Some can find it difficult to physically love another person. Virgo Moons can be very critical of other people and of themselves and can become fussy and nagging.

Moon in Libra:

Moon in Libra people are generally attractive, harmonious and charming. People like them and they are popular amongst others. They rarely argue and are capable of seeing both sides of any situation, for this reason they are sought after as confidantes.

Libra Moons are thoughtful, compassionate and loving and are unwilling to cause anyone pain or to upset them. They often get hurt themselves as they hate any disharmony or conflict. In fact they will run away from a situation that they feel is brewing rather than face it. They are accomplished side-steppers. Choices and decisions are difficult to make and a Libra Moon will agonise long and hard before reaching a conclusion, and then is beset by fears that the conclusion was not the correct one. They change their minds with great frequency. Libra Moons have a deep love of beauty, art and music and their surroundings must be pleasant and harmonious in order for them to be contented.

In love Libra Moons will be gentle and quietly passionate if not very innovative. They tend to be rather undemanding in general, although they have a need to be liked by other people and to be accepted.

Moon in Scorpio:

Scorpio Moons are ambitious, creative and highly charged emotionally. They do nothing by halves, putting their all into everything they attempt. They can be extremist in their attitudes up to the point of fanaticism. They have a will of iron and once their teeth are sunk into something they will never let go. Sexually, they are intense and highly geared towards the sensual and erotic. Sexual gratification is important to them and this is charged by their immense power of imagination.

Scorpio Moons will rarely share their innermost feelings with anyone else. Their secrets remain their own and they tell other people only what they deliberately want them to know, there is little spontaneous soul-sharing. Most Scorpio Moons would prefer to work alone and they have tremendous powers of concentration. They never really need the help or assistance of other people being very capable of sorting out their own problems.

Although Scorpio Moons are very secretive about their own affairs they do like to uncover and know the secrets of other people. They are excellent detectives and will root skeletons out of other's cupboards with unerring accuracy.

Scorpio Moons can be susceptible to the influence of drink and drugs more than the average person would be. They are very drawn to sensation and feelings, liking to experience everything there is to experience in life. In some, perversion takes the place of sensuality.

Moon in Sagittarius

Sagittarius Moons like to entertain other people and to make them laugh. They are generally very cheerful people, always ready for a joke and to share their time with friends. Very sociable in outlook, friends and companions are very important to them. Sagittarius Moons enjoy nothing more than a long evening discussing philosophy and changing the world. They thrive on conversation and geniality.

Tact is not a strong virtue, they will often unwittingly hurt other people by saying the wrong thing at the wrong time. Patience is never a virtue, they will rush headlong into any hare-brained scheme which appeals to them and often fall flat on their faces in the process. However, they just pick themselves up and start again, rarely learning from their past mistakes. Luck always seems to follow them and even the worst laid plans seem to turn out right for the Sagittarian Moon.

Sport and outdoor interests appeal strongly and there is a need for physical activity and to keep reasonably fit. Sagittarian Moons would atrophy if they had to sit down for long periods of time, they like to come and go as they please and dislike other people giving them orders. Sagittarian Moon people do not make the most satisfactory marriage partners; they need their freedom too much and hate to feel trapped or smothered.

Moon in Capricorn

The Moon in Capricorn is quite a difficult combination; Capricorn being a very practical and authoritarian sign. Moon in Capricorn people tend mainly to be rather cold, undemonstrative and ruthless. These people are not impressionable, life is carefully planned and calculated rather than flowing naturally.

Moon in Capricorn people are usually successful in business and career, although some make many enemies through their lack of compassion and feelings for others. They are often shy underneath their hard exterior and this shyness comes out as standoffishness. Love and affection are not given easily and a Capricorn Moon must try hard to overcome this and try to relate with other people more freely and openly.

Capricorn Moons are dependable and forthright and will choose for their life-partner, someone who shares these qualities. Capricorn Moons expect a great deal from their partner in the way of support, encouragement and practicality. They do not suffer fools at all and tend to look down on lesser mortals with disdain.

Moon in Aquarius

Moon in Aquarius people are free thinkers who hate to be tied down into domesticity. Although they are quite capable of faithfulness it is not easy for them to accomplish. Aquarian Moons are not built to be enclosed by rules and regulations, they need to think and discuss their ideas and thoughts with other people.

Many Aquarian Moon people are gifted in one way or another, some to the point of genius. Their far-sighted ideas and vision is unique. They are very humanitarian and really care about their 'causes'. This is not affectation, but very real and necessary for them. There is a deep need to change the world and make it a better place for everyone and everything, human, animal or vegetable. Many Aquarian Moons are rather eccentric and 'different' both in outlook and in manner, yet they make friends easily and are popular with other people, working and relating well and efficiently with groups and organisations. They have a strong need to change and reform things which they feel are wrong or unfair. Many are drawn to occult or 'new age' studies and have talent in these areas.

Moon in Pisces

Moon in Pisces people are sensitive, emotional and ruled by their feelings. They often live in a dream-world of their own making, preferring this to the horrors and disappointments of real life. They are much given to fantasy and imagination. They are amusing and interesting as friends but are not easy to live with unless they are really loved by their partner.

Pisces Moons are generally very psychic and intuitive, sometimes to the extent that they find it hard to separate what is real and what is not. They are subjected to many varied mood swings and can deviate from elation to utter misery in the space of a few moments. The duality of the sign causes the Pisces Moon person to change from quiet, retrospective, helpless victim into a wild, party animal who craves stimulating company with alarming speed. Pisces Moons are usually well-liked, friendly, kind, generous and quiet - they are also infuriating at times. It is very easy for other people to take unfair advantage and they must beware of trusting everyone on sight through their almost childlike trust and innocence.

Pisces Moon people love art and music - anything that is beautiful and gentle in fact. As with the Scorpio Moon, Pisces Moons are very susceptible to the effects of drugs and alcohol. Addictions are a possibility which should be guarded against.

Moon Journey

You are walking along a pathway which runs through the centre of a large forest. The path is wide, straight and feels firm yet sandy under your feet. Dusk is gathering and the evening is rich with the twitterings of settling birds as they prepare to roost amongst the trees on either side of you. The air is warm upon your skin and you feel safe, contented and secure.

You are happy in your walk, just you, the trees and the sky above you. You notice a small clearing to your left and sit down for a while to rest on the soft, green grass which is growing there. A warren of rabbits emerge from a burrow to your right and you watch them as they feed and play together. You are drowsily content to lie in your clearing and watch the world go by as you attune yourself with life and nature.

Night slowly begins to fall and you catch sight of the rising Moon hovering behind the trees in front of you. You stand up, regain the pathway, and walk on, feeling the stillness of the night surrounding you. An owl hoots from an ancient ash tree, an eerie and melancholy sound. The Moon, now rising above the pathway glows larger and brighter against the night sky and you quicken your steps. She seems to be calling you and you instinctively answer the call.

You begin to run, faster and faster along the path, feeling energised and exhilarated. Your feet are flying over the sandy ground. The path begins to bend and you slow down again to a trot. You round the turn and see running ahead of you, a hare. She pauses, looks at you, and leaps away again. You know that she is leading you and you are content to follow her. The pathway continues for some distance until you reach a stile; the hare passes underneath it and you climb over.

In front of you is a huge sand dune, dotted with swathes of marram grass. The hare is sitting quietly on the top of the dune. You ascend the dune, your feet slipping slightly in the soft sand. The hare does not move or run away. When you reach the top you can see a short expanse of beach and the sea glistening behind it. The water looks calm and black on this windless night. The Moon, now large and full casts a silvery path of moonlight upon the water. The vision of this is heartstoppingly beautiful. You walk on, past the hare, and head towards the sea. At the waters edge the moonpath beckons.

Your clothes are suddenly gone and you enter the water. The coldness of it as it surrounds your feet causes you to shiver and gooseflesh to envelop your skin. You wade on until the water reaches your knees, then your thighs, then your hips. You gradually acclimatise to the chill of the sea. Now the water feels cool and refreshing, rather than cold. You begin to swim gently along the moonpath towards the glowing orb of the Moon. After a few minutes you stop swimming and begin to float on your back. The water supports you gently and you feel safe and secure. Nothing can harm you here. Gently you feel your consciousness rising from your body and ascending towards the Moon.

You have no fear and are willing to accept whatever is to happen. You feel yourself floating gently upwards as if attached to silver ribbons of light. At last you stop your ascent and find that you are standing before a silver gate, which opens to you. You walk through it and see that everything in this place is silver or black. Here there is also a beach, of silver sand dotted with shells and crystals. The ocean is as black as jet ,glinting with silvery speckles of light. You begin to walk along the beach, picking up and putting down a crystal or shell here and there.

In the distance you see a woman moving towards you. Her walk is graceful and fluid and she is holding out her hands to you as she approaches. You are suddenly overcome with emotion and drop to your knees as she reaches you. You can feel the waves of love envelop you as she reaches down and lifts you back to your feet. This the Goddess and she takes your hand and begins to lead you along the beach. Open yourself to her and allow her to communicate with you. What she has to say is personal to you. Listen and remember her words.

Some time should now be spent in communication with the Goddess of the Moon.

You offer your farewells to the Goddess, thanking her for the time she has given you. You then begin to retrace your steps along the beach until you reach the silver gate. You can feel something in your hand and when you look you will find there a symbol, a gift from the Moon Mother. Take this and treasure it. You close your eyes and find yourself drifting back towards the sea beneath you. You can see your body floating gently on the smooth water.

You return to your body, slipping quietly back into yourself. As your consciousness awakens you slowly begin to swim back to the shore. As you leave the water you allow the warm air to dry you before dressing in your clothes which are lying on the beach. You retrace your steps towards the sand dune and then climb it once more. The hare is still sitting at the top, quietly watching you. As you pass by, she leaps into the shadows beyond the dune and you see her no more. You once more begin to follow the path back into your own place and time. The journey is over.

The Lunar Calendar

The Moon has probably been used as a calendar since man's consciousness was first awakened. Unlike the constant journeying of the Sun which is seasonal, the Moon's ever-changing monthly cycles are clearly visible for everyone to see. The Moon provides a natural calculator which everyone can read upon sight. One complete cycle of the Moon's phases takes approximately 29 days to complete. The term 'month' derives from 'moonth' the period of one complete lunation from Full Moon to Full Moon.

The Islamic calendar is still calculated by the phases of the Moon rather than the Sun. It is effective, although it does tend, in time, to become out of line with the seasons.

Witches and Pagans use a Lunar Calendar to arrange their meetings and gatherings by. The Esbat, or Full Moon meetings are held monthly. These are the 'lesser' gatherings, where the business of the coven is organised and spells, healings and practical work is undertaken. Some covens also hold Esbat meetings at the New Moon in addition to the Full Moon. Esbat workings are very important to Witches and Pagans as the face of the Goddess, The Great Mother is reflected in the Moon. The Moon is her sign and symbol. Her power and influence is manifested on Earth through the well-being and contentment of mankind, the sturdy growth of crops and in the health of animals.

The Goddess has three faces which mirror the phases of the Moon. At the New to Waxing Moon, she is a young virgin who is just feeling the first stirrings of sexual awakening. At the Full Moon she is a mature woman, sexually ripe and fertile. At the Waning and Dark Moon she is an ancient hag or crone, sterile but very wise. Yet all are one and She is called the Threefold Goddess.

The Esbats fall, generally, in between the four Great Sabbats (Imbolg, Beltaine, Lughnasad and Samhain) and the four Lesser Sabbats (Vernal or Spring Equinox, Summer Solstice, Autumn Equinox and Winter Solstice) The four Lesser Sabbats are solar rather than lunar. On occasion, the Full Moon Esbat coincides with a Sabbat.

The date of Easter Sunday is still calculated by the Pagan lunar calendar. Easter always falls on the first Sunday after the first Full Moon after the Vernal Equinox. The date of Easter, therefore, varies quite considerably from year to year, sometimes falling in March, sometimes in April.

The Nightingale Moon falls between the end of April and mid May, at the time when the nightingales migrate to Britain to breed. The Honey Moon, which is large and honey-coloured, is the Full Moon closest to the Summer Solstice. The Harvest Moon is the Full Moon which falls closest to the Autumn Equinox. The Hunters Moon is the next Full Moon which follows it.

The Anglo-Saxon Moonth/ Calendar is listed overleaf.

Anglo-Saxon Moonth/ Calendar

JANUARY: Wulf-monath, the month of wolves

FEBRUARY: Sprote-cal, the month of kale (a type of cabbage)

MARCH: Hreth-monath, the rough month

APRIL: Eoestra-monath, the month of Easter

MAY: Tri-milchi, the month when the cows are milked three times a day

JUNE: Sere-monath, the dry month

JULY: Maed-monath, the meadow month

AUGUST: Weod-monath, the month of vegetation

SEPTEMBER: Haerfest-monath, the harvest month

OCTOBER: Win-monath, the month of wine

NOVEMBER: Wind-monath, the month of wind

DECEMBER: Mid-Winter-monath, the month of Mid-Winter

The Menstruating Moon

Women fall into two distinct categories during their fertile years. The Virgin Mary archetype and the Mary Magdalene archetype (or the innocent and the tart). Mary the Virgin gave birth without first having sex, whereas Mary Magdalene had sex without giving birth.

Eve and Lilith are similar in their persuasion: Eve gave birth to Cain and Abel... sex for the purpose of procreation. Pure, wholesome and clean (Unless you consider the fact that as Eve was the only woman, Cain and Abel had to have incestuous sex with her in order to procreate their own children, but that is beside the point). Lilith was considered to be a succubus, a purely sexual, therefore evil creature. She had no children... she bled, therefore, she was unclean and dangerous.

Throughout the ages and throughout countless cultures and 'civilisations' the menstruating woman has been considered to be dangerous and unclean. She becomes a creature to be segregated from the rest of the community. In some of the more primitive cultures she is forced to live apart from her family/tribe for the duration of her 'moon time'.

Ancient superstition and fear die hard and painfully slowly. In the days of our earliest civilisation, it had to be noticed that women bled. A woman could bleed, yet she did not die. This is and was the woman's mystery. The issue of menstrual blood, without a wound, without agony and without possible death was a marvel to be feared and respected by men.

A woman could also magically produce life from her body. Not only could she reproduce a likeness of herself, she could produce male children as well. A sexual coupling which had taken place nine months beforehand was unlikely to have been considered as relevant to the event of childbirth. Therefore, women had magical powers which men did not have and did not understand.

As with all things that humans do not understand, menstruation equalled power and therefore was evil and must be hidden away. Even today many women segregate themselves during menstruation, avoiding all sexual contact, so as not to 'offend' their husband or partner. The period is still looked upon as a 'curse' rather than a part of the natural rhythm of the female cycle.

The menstrual cycle of women is on average of 28/29 days duration. The Moon goes through her complete lunation in approximately the same time. For this reason the time of a woman's bleeding has been known as her 'Moon time'.

The term 'menstrual cycle' derives from the Latin mens, mensis meaning 'month' the word 'month' derives from 'moonth' and in turn means 'moon' The word 'month' also means 'measure'. 'Menstruation' is also referred to as 'measure' so therefore 'menstruation' comes from 'month' which in turn comes from 'Moon'.

There is polarity between ovulation and menstruation. Ovulation occurring half way through the monthly cycle. The cycle of the Moon mirrors this in the time span between Full Moon and New Moon or First Quarter Moon to Last Quarter Moon. The period from New Moon to New Moon averages out at about 4 weeks. 29.53 days (mean synodic month).

It has been noticed that women who live, work or socialise together will more often than not, bleed together also. I have found this to be true amongst my own circle of friends and myself. The more time we spend together, the more we become synchronised into a very similar cycle of bleeding, PMS, bleeding, etc. Women who are close share a natural rhythmic pattern which draws them even closer together, both mentally and physically.

Men have no such natural patterns, and maybe this would explain why female friendships are usually very much more emotionally satisfying, comfortable and tactile than male to male friendships would generally appear to be. Women are not afraid to be seen to be very close to another woman.

Bibliography

Oxford Dictionary of Nursery Rhymes, Iona & Peter Opie (1951) Oxford University Press.

Meals Medicinal with Herbal Simples, W.D. Fernie, M.D. (1905) John Wright & Co. Bristol.

The Shell Country Book, Geoffrey Grigson (1962) Pheonix House Ltd., London.

The American Ephemeris for the 20th Century, Neil F. Michelsen (1980) ACS Publications, California.

The Wise Wound (Menstruation and Everywoman) Penelope Shuttle and Peter Redgrove. Paladin, London. 1986.

The New Larousse Encyclopedia of Mythology. Translated by Richard Aldington and Delana Ames. Hamlyn Publishing. 1959. (Edition used 1986).

Inanna, Queen of Heaven and Earth. Diane Wolkstein and Samuel Noah Kramer. Rider 1984.

Aspects of Occultism. Dion Fortune. Aquarian Press. 1982 edition.

The Year of the Goddess. Lawrence Durdin-Robertson. Aquarian Press 1990.

Earth Dance - A Year of Pagan Rituals. Jan Brodie. Capall Bann 1995.

Mysteries of Space. Patrick Moore. Armada 1979.

Women's Mysteries. M. Esther Harding. Rider 1989.

The Gardeners Folklore. Margaret Baker. David & Charles 1977.

Tables of Moon Phases 1996-1999

Moon Phases 1996

January
Full Moon	5th January	20.51pm	14'48 Cancer
Last Quarter	13th January	20.45pm	22'57 Libra
New Moon	20th January	12.51pm	29'45 Capricorn
First Quarter	27th January	11.14am	06'48 Taurus

February
Full Moon	4th February	15.58pm	15'07 Leo
Last Quarter	12th February	08.37am	22'55 Scorpio
New Moon	18th February	23.30pm	29'36 Aquarius
First Quarter	26th February	05.52am	06'55 Gemini

March
Full Moon	5th March	09.23am	15'06 Virgo
Last Quarter	12th March	17.15pm	22'25 Sagittarius
New Moon	19th March	10.45am	29'07 Pisces
First Quarter	27th March	01.31am	06'40 Cancer

April

Full Moon	4th April	00.07am	14'31 Libra
Last Quarter	10th April	23.36pm	21'22 Capricorn
New Moon	17th April	22.49pm	28'12 Aries
First Quarter	25th April	20.40pm	05'55 Leo

May

Full Moon	3rd May	11.48am	13'19 Scorpio
Last Quarter	10th May	05.04am	19'49 Aquarius
New Moon	17th May	11.46am	26'51 Taurus
First Quarter	25th May	14.13pm	04'38 Virgo

June

Full Moon	1st June	20.47pm	11'37 Sagittarius
Last Quarter	8th June	11.06am	17'56 Pisces
New Moon	16th June	01.36am	25'12 Gemini
First Quarter	24th June	05.23am	02'59 Libra

July

Full Moon	1st July	03.58am	09'36 Capricorn
Last Quarter	7th July	18.55pm	15'55 Aries
New Moon	15th July	16.15pm	23'26 Cancer
First Quarter	23rd July	17.49pm	01'08 Scorpio
Full Moon	30th July	10.35am	07'32 Aquarius

August

Last Quarter	6th August	05.25am	14'02 Taurus
New Moon	14th August	07.34am	21'47 Leo
First Quarter	22nd August	03.36am	29'20 Scorpio
Full Moon	28th August	17.52pm	05'41 Pisces

September

Last Quarter	4th September	19.06pm	12'31 Gemini
New Moon	12th September	23.07pm	20'27 Virgo
First Quarter	20th September	11.23am	27'46 Sagittarius
Full Moon	27th September	02.51am	04'17 Aries

October

Last Quarter	4th October	12.04pm	11'32 Cancer
New Moon	12th October	14.14pm	19'32 Libra
First Quarter	19th October	18.09pm	26'38 Capricorn
Full Moon	26th October	14.11pm	03'26 Taurus

November

Last Quarter	3rd November	07.50am	11'10 Leo
New Moon	11th November	04.16am	19'03 Scorpio
First Quarter	18th November	01.09am	25'59 Aquarius
Full Moon	25th November	04.10am	03'10 Gemini

December

Last Quarter	3rd December	05.06am	11'19 Virgo
New Moon	10th December	16.56pm	18'56 Sagittarius
First Quarter	17th December	09.31am	25'44 Pisces
Full Moon	24th December	20.41pm	03'20 Cancer

Moon Phases 1997

January

Last Quarter	2nd January	01.45am	11'42 Libra
New Moon	9th January	04.26am	18'57 Capricorn
First Quarter	15th January	20.02pm	25'44 Aries
Full Moon	23rd January	15.11pm	03'40 Leo
Last Quarter	31st January	19.40pm	11'59 Scorpio

February

New Moon	7th February	15.06pm	18'53 Aquarius
First Quarter	14th February	08.58am	25'43 Taurus
Full Moon	22nd February	10.27am	03'51 Virgo

March

Last Quarter	2nd March	09.38am	11'51 Sagittarius
New Moon	9th March	01.15am	18'31 Pisces
First Quarter	16th March	00.06am	25'27 Gemini
Full Moon	24th March	04.45am	03'35 Libra
Last Quarter	31st March	19.38pm	11'08 Capricorn

April

New Moon	7th April	11.02am	17'40 Aries
First Quarter	14th April	17.00pm	24'47 Cancer
Full Moon	22nd April	20.03pm	02'45 Scorpio
Last Quarter	30th April	02.37am	09'48 Aquarius

May

New Moon	6th May	20.47pm	16'21 Taurus
First Quarter	14th May	10.55am	23'41 Leo
Full Moon	22nd May	09.13am	01'19 Sagittarius
Last Quarter	29th May	07.51am	07'59 Pisces

June

New Moon	5th June	07.04am	14'40 Gemini
First Quarter	13th June	04.52am	22'14 Virgo
Full Moon	20th June	19.09pm	29'29 Sagittarius
Last Quarter	27th June	12.42pm	05'54 Aries

July

New Moon	4th July	18.40pm	12'48 Cancer
First Quarter	12th July	21.44pm	20'34 Libra
Full Moon	20th July	03.20am	27'28 Capricorn
Last Quarter	26th July	18.28pm	03'47 Taurus

August

New Moon	3rd August	08.14am	11'02 Leo
First Quarter	11th August	12.42pm	18'53 Scorpio
Full Moon	18th August	10.55am	25'32 Aquarius
Last Quarter	25th August	02.24am	01'56 Gemini

September

New Moon	1st September	23.52pm	09'34 Virgo
First Quarter	10th September	01.31am	17'23 Sagittarius
Full Moon	16th September	18.51pm	23'56 Pisces
Last Quarter	23rd September	13.35pm	00'33 Cancer

October

New Moon	1st October	16.52pm	08'33 Libra
First Quarter	9th October	12.22pm	16'15 Capricorn
Full Moon	16th October	03.46am	22'49 Aries
Last Quarter	23rd October	04.48am	29'49 Cancer
New Moon	31st October	10.01am	08'01 Scorpio

November

First Quarter	7th November	21.43pm	15'31 Aquarius
Full Moon	14th November	14.12pm	22'15 Taurus
Last Quarter	21st November	23.58pm	29'43 Leo
New Moon	30th November	02.14am	07'54 Sagittarius

December

First Quarter	7th December	06.09am	15'10 Pisces
Full Moon	14th December	02,37am	22'08 Gemini
Last Quarter	21st December	21.43pm	00'04 Libra
New Moon	29th December	16.57pm	08'01 Capricorn

Moon Phases 1998

January

First Quarter	5th January	14.18pm	15'03 Aries
Full Moon	12th January	17.24pm	22'18 Cancer
Last Quarter	20th January	19.20pm	00'33 Scorpio
New Moon	28th January	06.01am	08'06 Aquarius

February

First Quarter	3rd February	22.53pm	14'55 Taurus
Full Moon	11th February	10.23am	22'29 Leo
Last Quarter	19th February	15.27pm	00'47 Sagittarius
New Moon	26th February	17.26pm	07'55 Pisces

March

First Quarter	5th March	08.41am	14'34 Gemini
Full Moon	13th March	04.34am	22'24 Virgo
Last Quarter	21st March	07.38am	00'29 Capricorn
New Moon	28th March	03.14am	07'15 Aries

April

First Quarter	3rd April	20.18pm	13'52 Cancer
Full Moon	11th April	22.24pm	21'49 Libra
Last Quarter	19th April	19'53pm	29'33 Capricorn
New Moon	26th April	11.41am	06'03 Taurus

May

First Quarter	3rd May	10.04am	12'47 Leo
Full Moon	11th May	14.29pm	20'42 Virgo
Last Quarter	19th May	04.35am	28'01 Aquarius
New Moon	25th May	19.32pm	04'23 Gemini

June

First Quarter	2nd June	01.45am	11'21 Virgo
Full Moon	10th June	04.18am	19'06 Sagittarius
Last Quarter	17th June	10.38am	26'03 Pisces
New Moon	24th June	03.50am	02'27 Cancer

July

First Quarter	1st July	18.43pm	09'44 Libra
Full Moon	9th July	16.01pm	17'15 Capricorn
Last Quarter	16th July	15.13pm	23'53 Aries
New Moon	23rd July	13.44pm	00'31 Leo
First Quarter	31st July	12.05pm	08'05 Scorpio

August

Full Moon	8th August	02.10am	15'21 Aquarius
Last Quarter	14th August	19.49pm	21'49 Taurus
New Moon	22nd August	02.03am	28'48 Leo
First Quarter	30th August	05.07am	06'38 Sagittarius

September

Full Moon	6th September	11.21am	13'40 Pisces
Last Quarter	13th September	01.58am	20'05 Gemini
New Moon	20th September	17.02pm	27'32 Virgo
First Quarter	28th September	21.11pm	05'32 Capricorn

October

Full Moon	5th October	20.12pm	12'23 Aries
Last Quarter	12th October	11.11am	18'55 Cancer
New Moon	20th October	10.09am	26'49 Libra
First Quarter	28th October	11.46am	04'51 Aquarius

November

Full Moon	4th November	05.18am	11'35 Taurus
Last Quarter	11th November	00.28am	18'24 Leo
New Moon	19th November	04.27am	26'38 Scorpio
First Quarter	27th November	00.23am	04'33 Pisces

December

Full Moon	3rd December	15.19pm	11'15 Gemini
Last Quarter	10th December	17.54pm	18'28 Virgo
New Moon	18th December	2.42pm	26'48 Sagittarius
First Quarter	6th December	10.46am	04'27 Aries

Moon Phases 1999

January
Full Moon	2nd January	02.50am	11'15 Cancer
Last Quarter	9th January	14.22pm	18'52 Libra
New Moon	17th January	15.46pm	27'05 Capricorn
First Quarter	24th January	19.15pm	04'21 Taurus
Full Moon	31st January	16.07pm	11'20 Leo

February
Last Quarter	8th February	11.58pm	19'16 Scorpio
New Moon	16th February	06.39am	27'08 Aquarius
First Quarter	23rd February	02.43am	04'02 Gemini

March
Full Moon	2nd March	06.59am	11.15 Virgo
Last Quarter	10th March	08.40am	19'19 Sagittarius
New Moon	17th March	18.48pm	26'44 Pisces
First Quarter	24th March	10.18am	03'20 Cancer
Full Moon	31st March	22.49pm	10'46 Libra

April
Last Quarter	9th April	02.51am	18'49 Capricorn
New Moon	16th April	04.22am	25'45 Aries
First Quarter	22nd April	19.02pm	02'12 Leo
Full Moon	30th April	14.55pm	09'49 Scorpio

May

Last Quarter	8th May	17.29pm	17'41 Aquarius
New Moon	15th May	12.05pm	24'14 Taurus
First Quarter	22nd May	05.34am	00'43 Virgo
Full Moon	30th May	06.40am	08'26 Sagittarius

June

Last Quarter	7th June	04.20am	16'00 Pisces
New Moon	13th June	19.03pm	22'20 Gemini
First Quarter	20th June	18.13pm	28'59 Virgo
Full Moon	28th June	21.38pm	06'45 Capricorn

July

Last Quarter	6th July	11.57am	13'59 Aries
New Moon	13th July	02.24am	20'17 Cancer
First Quarter	20th July	09.00am	27'14 Libra
Full Moon	28th July	11.25am	04'58 Aquarius

August

Last Quarter	4th August	17.27pm	11'54 Taurus
New Moon	11th August	11.09am	18'21 Leo
First Quarter	19th August	01.47am	25'40 Scorpio
Full Moon	26th August	23.48pm	03'17 Pisces

September

Last Quarter	2nd September	22.17pm	10'00 Gemini
New Moon	9th September	22.02pm	16'47 Virgo
First Quarter	17th September	20.06pm	24'29 Sagittarius
Full Moon	25th September	10.51am	01'56 Aries

October

Last Quarter	2nd October	04.02am	08'31 Cancer
New Moon	9th October	11.34am	15'44 Libra
First Quarter	17th October	15.00pm	23'48 Capricorn
Full Moon	24th October	21.02pm	01'00 Taurus
Last Quarter	31st October	12.04pm	07'37 Leo

November

New Moon	8th November	03.53am	15'07 Scorpio
First Quarter	16th November	09.03am	23'33 Aquarius
Full Moon	23rd November	07.04am	00'32 Gemini
Last Quarter	29th November	23.19pm	07'17 Virgo

December

New Moon	7th December	22.32pm	15'22 Sagittarius
First Quarter	16th December	00.50am	23'36 Pisces
Full Moon	22nd December	17.31pm	00'25 Cancer
Last Quarter	29th December	14.04pm	07'24 Libra

Index

FREE DETAILED CATALOGUE

A detailed illustrated catalogue is available on request, SAE or International Postal Coupon appreciated. **Titles are available direct from Capall Bann, post free in the UK** (cheque or PO with order) and ar available from good bookshops and specialist outlets. Well over 100 titles in print including:

Arthur - The Legend Unveiled by C Johnson & E Lung
Auguries and Omens - The Magical Lore of Birds by Yvonne Aburrow
Book of the Veil The by Peter Paddon
Call of the Horned Piper by Nigel Jackson
Cats' Company by Ann Walker
Celtic Lore & Druidic Ritual by Rhiannon Ryall
Compleat Vampyre - The Vampyre Shaman: Werewolves & Witchery by Nigel Jackson
Crystal Clear - A Guide to Quartz Crystal by Jennifer Dent
Earth Dance - A Year of Pagan Rituals by Jan Brodie
Earth Magic by Margaret McArthur
Enchanted Forest - The Magical Lore of Trees by Yvonne Aburrow
Healing Homes by Jennifer Dent
Herbcraft - Shamanic & Ritual Use of Herbs by Susan Lavender & Anna Franklin
In Search of Herne the Hunter by Eric Fitch
Inner Space Workbook - Developing Counselling & Magical Skills Through the Tarot
Kecks, Keddles & Kesh by Michael Bayley
Living Tarot by Ann Walker
Magical Lore of Cats by Marion Davies
Magical Lore of Herbs by Marion Davies
Masks of Misrule - The Horned God & His Cult in Europe by Nigel Jackson
Mysteries of the Runes by Michael Howard
Patchwork of Magic by Julia Day
Pathworking - A Practical Book of Guided Meditations by Pete Jennings
Pickingill Papers - The Origins of Gardnerian Wicca by Michael Howard
Psychic Self Defence - Real Solutions by Jan Brodie
Runic Astrology by Nigel Pennick
Sacred Animals by Gordon 'The Toad' Maclellan
Sacred Grove - The Mysteries of the Forest by Yvonne Aburrow
Sacred Geometry by Nigel Pennick
Sacred Lore of Horses The by Marion Davies
Sacred Ring - Pagan Origins British Folk Festivals & Customs by Michael Howard
Secret Places of the Goddess by Philip Heselton
Talking to the Earth by Gordon Maclellan
The Goddess Year by Nigel Pennick & Helen Field
West Country Wicca by Rhiannon Ryall
Wildwood King by Philip Kane
Witches of Oz The by Matthew & Julia Phillips

Capall Bann is owned and run by people actively involved in many of the areas in which we publish. Our list is expanding rapidly so do contact us for details on the latest releases. We guarantee our mailing list will never be released to other companies or organisations.

Capall Bann Publishing, Freshfields, Chieveley, Berks, RG20 8TF.